ELECTRIC UNDERGROUND -A CITY LIGHTS READER

ELECTRIC UNDERGROUND -A CITY LIGHTS READER

NEW ENGLISH LIBRARY

TIMES MIRROR

First I must acknowledge the enthusiasm of Lawrence Ferlinghetti, who really is "City Lights". Also the original idea for this collection which came from Peter Haining.

Introduction © Laurence James 1973
Extract from "The White Negro" © Dissent Publishing Associates, 1957
Extract from "Eco-Catastrophe" © Dr. Paul Erlich, 1969
May Day Speech © City Lights Books, 1970
"In Defense of Jayne Mansfield" from "Meat Science Essays" © Michael McClure, 1963, 1966
"Pound At Spoleto" © City Lights Books, 1966
Extract from "Boy With Face Of Sour Apples" © City Lights Books, 1966
Extract from "First Third" © City Lights Books, 1964
Extract from "Trout Fishing In America" © City Lights Books, 1963
"I Am Dying, Meester?" © City Lights Books, 1963
"Hymn To The Goddess San Francisco In Paradise" © City Lights Books, 1964
"Daily Life" © City Lights Books, 1964
"Mad Sonnet" © City Lights Books, 1966
"Shag" © City Lights Books, 1966
"Suicide Note" © City Lights Books, 1963
"There's An Old Story" © City Lights Books, 1963
"Theology" © City Lights Books, 1964
"The Fog" © City Lights Books, 1964
"A Questionnaire" © City Lights Books, 1963
"Flowers And Bullets" © City Lights Books, 1970
Jack Kerouac poetry from "Scattered Poems" © Jack Kerouac, 1956, 1959, 1967
Allen Ginsberg poetry from "Howl And Other Poems" © Allen Ginsberg, 1956, 1959
Pablo Picasso Poetry from "Hunks Of Skin"—English Translations © Paul Blackburn, 1968
Philip Lamantia Poetry from "Selected Poems" © Philip Lamantia, 1967
Lawrence Ferlinghetti Poetry from "Pictures Of The Gone World" © Lawrence Ferlinghetti, 1955
Poetry of Voznesensky, Kirsanov, and "Babi Yar" and "Uriah Heep" by Yevtushenko are from "Red Cats", English Versions © Anselm Hollo, 1962
The following poems of Gregory Corso are from "Gasoline":
    "I Am 25", "Last Night I Drove A Car", "The Last Warmth of Arnold", "The Last Gangster", "D. Scarlatti" and "Puma In Chapultepec Zoo" © Gregory Corso, 1958
The following poems of Gregory Corso are from "Vestal Lady on Brattle":
    "The Wreck Of The Nordling", "Dementia In An African Apartment House", "In The Early Morning", "Sea Chanty", "A Pastoral Fetish" and "Greenwich Village Suicide" © Gregory Corso, 1955

The English distributors for all City Lights Books are: McBride and Broadley Ltd., 9 Nash Road, Great Horwood (Near Bletchley) MK17 ORA.

This collection first published anywhere in the world by New English Library, Barnard's Inn, Holborn, London E.C.1. in 1973.

Printed in Great Britain by C. Tinling & Co., London and Prescot.

450016021

CONTENTS

5

INTRODUCTION

Laurence James

This collection is dedicated to the fond memory of 'Wholly Communion', celebrated at the Royal Albert Hall in June, 1965.

Right at the very beginning of the sixties I was working in a large bookshop in Charing Cross Road. My predecessor had bequeathed to me a small, pocket-sized volume of poems called 'Kaddish', by an American writer – Allen Ginsberg. It was published under the imprint of a small San Francisco firm named 'City Lights'. At the time, I hadn't heard of either the writer or the publisher, and the book didn't look all that interesting. However, during a tedious period when I had nothing to pre-occupy me – apart from imagining what luxuries I might purchase with my salary of eight pounds per week – I opened 'Kaddish' and began reading.

Trite clichés like 'mind-blowing' can only convey a fraction of the effect of that poetry. Although there were shades of Whitman, it had a truly fantastic freshness. From Ginsberg I found my way to the picaresque novels of Jack Kerouac which showed me the open roads of America better than any travel guide. After Kerouac I read into the whole world of American 'beat' writing, in all its splendour.

I personally owe City Lights an enormous debt of gratitude, and I am delighted to have the opportunity of putting this anthology together – almost as a sort of tribute – and so giving other people a chance to taste the flavour of this unique and lively publishing house.

For newcomers to City Lights, this is a reasonably representative collection of some of the best. For the reader who is already familiar with the imprint, there are some of the biggest names, and one or two lesser known pieces, so it can be a voyage of both nostalgia and exploration.

I must stress that this is a personal collection. Nothing is here that I don't personally like very much. It's not the 'best' or the 'newest' or the 'greatest'. There's some prose, and some fine poetry. Incidentally, most of the books that I've drawn from are still available, so if any of my selections happen to strike a chord, it's easy for you to follow them up.

I don't want to go through the contents lists and comment on it piece by piece. I must draw your attention to the brief extract from Neal Cassady's 'First Third' – a crucial and vastly influential novel. Then there's the bitter polemic of Genet – the wry genius of William Burroughs – Ginsberg's apocalyptic vision of America – the poetry of Kerouac, Ferlinghetti and Corso – I could easily go on for pages – Mailer, Ehrlich, Brautigan, Picasso, Yevtushenko and many more!

If an award was ever given for something important, like the most influential publishers of literature anywhere in the world, there'd be no justice if it didn't go to Lawrence Ferlinghetti in San Francisco.

Laurence James,
Stanstead Abbotts,
Hertfordshire.
July, 1973.

IN THE BAGGAGE ROOM AT GREYHOUND

Allen Ginsberg

I

In the depths of the Greyhound Terminal
sitting dumbly on a baggage truck looking at the sky waiting for
    the Los Angeles Express to depart
worrying about eternity over the Post Office roof in the night-time
    red downtown heaven,
staring through my eyeglasses I realized shuddering these thoughts
    were not eternity, nor the poverty of our lives, irritable
    baggage clerks,
nor the millions of weeping relatives surrounding the buses waving
    goodbye,
nor other millions of the poor rushing around from city to city to
    see their loved ones,
nor an indian dead with fright talking to a huge cop by the Coke
    machine,
nor this trembling old lady with a cane taking the last trip of her
    life,
nor the red capped cynical porter collecting his quarters and
    smiling over the smashed baggage,
nor me looking around at the horrible dream,
nor mustached negro Operating Clerk named Spade, dealing out
    with his marvelous long hand the fate of thousands of express
    packages,
nor fairy Sam in the basement limping from leaden trunk to trunk,
nor Joe at the counter with his nervous breakdown smiling
    cowardly at the customers,
nor the grayish-green whale's stomach interior loft where we keep

9

the baggage in hideous racks,
hundreds of suitcases full of tragedy rocking back and forth
waiting to be opened,
nor the baggage that's lost, nor damaged handles, nameplates
vanished, busted wires & broken ropes, whole trunks exploding
on the concrete floor,
nor seabags emptied into the night in the final warehouse.

II

Yet Spade reminded me of Angel, unloading a bus,
dressed in blue overalls black face official Angel's workman cap,
pushing with his belly a huge tin horse piled high with black
baggage,
looking up he passed the yellow light bulb of the loft
and holding high on his arm an iron shepherd's crook.

III

It was the racks, I realized, sitting myself on top of them now as is
my wont at lunchtime to rest my tired foot,
it was the racks, great wooden shelves and stanchions posts and
beams assembled floor to roof jumbled with baggage,
—the Japanese white metal postwar trunk gaudily flowered &
headed for Fort Bragg,
one Mexican green paper package in purple rope adorned with
names for Nogales,
hundreds of radiators all at once for Eureka,
crates of Hawaiian underwear,
rolls of posters scattered over the Peninsula, nuts to Sacramento,
one human eye for Napa,
an aluminum box of human blood for Stockton
and a little red package of teeth for Calistoga —
it was the racks and these on the racks I saw naked in electric
light the night before I quit,
the racks were created to hang our possessions, to keep us
together, a temporary shift in space,
God's only way of building the rickety structure of Time,
to hold the bags to send on the roads, to carry our luggage from

place to place
looking for a bus to ride us back home to Eternity where the
heart was left and farewell tears began.

IV

A swarm of baggage sitting by the counter as the transcontinental
bus pulls in.
The clock registering 12.15 A.M., May 9, 1956, the second hand
moving forward, red.
.Getting ready to load my last bus. — Farewell, Walnut Creek
Richmond Vallejo Portland Pacific Highway
Fleet-footed Quicksilver, God of transience.
One last package sits lone at midnight sticking up out of the
Coast rack high as the dusty fluorescent light.

The wage they pay us is too low to live on. Tragedy reduced to
numbers.
This for the poor shepherds. I am a communist.

Farewell ye Greyhound where I suffered so much,
hurt my knee and scraped my hand and built my pectoral muscles
big as vagina.

I AM 25

Gregory Corso

With a love a madness for Shelley
Chatterton   Rimbaud
and the needy-yap of my youth
          has gone from ear to ear:
          I HATE OLD POETMEN!
Especially old poetmen who retract
who consult other old poetmen
who speak their youth in whispers,
saying:–I did those then
          but that was then
          that was then–
O I would quiet old men
say to them:–I am your friend
              what you once were, thru me
              you'll be again–
Then at night in the confidence of their homes
rip out their apology-tongues
              and steal their poems.

POEM

Jack Kerouac

Jazz killed itself
but don't let poetry kill itself

Dont be afraid
  of the cold night air

Dont listen to institutions
when you return manuscripts to
  brownstone

dont bow & scuffle
      for Edith Wharton pioneers
or ursula major nebraska prose
  just hang in your own backyard
    & laugh play pretty
      cake trombone
& if somebody give you beads
  juju, jew, or otherwise,

sleep with em around your neck

Your dreams'll maybe better

    There's no rain
      there's no me,
    I'm tellin ya man
      sure as shit.
1959

13

25

Lawrence Ferlinghetti

The world is a beautiful place
                                    to be born into
if you don't mind happiness
                          not always being
                                      so very much fun
      if you don't mind a touch of hell
                                now and then
            just when everything is fine
                                because even in heaven
                        they don't sing
                              all the time

      The world is a beautiful place
                                to be born into
        if you don't mind some people dying
                                  all the time
              or maybe only starving
                                some of the time
                which isn't half so bad
                            if it isn't you

Oh the world is a beautiful place
                              to be born into
          if you don't much mind
                          a few dead minds
              in the higher places
                          or a bomb or two
                  now and then
                          in your upturned faces

or such other improprieties
                        as our Name Brand society
                is prey to
                        with its men of distinction
        and its men of extinction
                        and its priests
            and other patrolmen

                            and its various segregations
    and congressional investigations
                        and other constipations
            that our fool flesh
                    is heir to
        Yes the world is the best place of all
                            for a lot of such things as
            making the fun scene
                    and making the love scene
    and making the sad scene
                    and singing low songs and having inspirations
        and walking around
                    looking at everything
                            and smelling flowers
        and goosing statues
                    and even thinking
                            and kissing people and
        making babies and wearing pants
                            and waving hats and
                    dancing
                            and going swimming in rivers
                    on picnics
                            in the middle of the summer
            and just generally
                    'living it up'

    Yes
        but then right in the middle of it
                            comes the smiling

                    mortician

SAN FRANCISCO CHRONICLE,
SUNDAY, MAY 24, 1970

RUSSIAN POET AND KENT STATE

MOSCOW

The leading Russian poet, Yevgeny Yevtushenko, has written a poem dedicated to 19-year-old Allison Krause, one of the four students killed by National Guard bullets at Kent State University campus on May 4.

The poem, 'Flowers and Bullets,' was printed in Pravda, the Communist party newspaper. Its theme was based on the report that the day before her death, Miss Krause had put a flower on a National Guardsman's rifle, saying that 'Flowers are better than bullets.'

Flowers & Bullets

Yevgeny Yevtushenko

Of course: Bullets don't like people
                        who love flowers.
They're jealous ladies, bullets,
                        short on kindness.
Allison Krause, nineteen years old,
                        you're dead,
for loving flowers.
When, thin and open as the pulse of conscience,
you put a flower in a rifle's mouth
                        and said,
'Flowers are better than bullets,'
                        that
was pure hope speaking.
Give no flowers to a state
                        that outlaws truth;
such states reciprocate
                        with cynical, cruel gifts,
and your gift, Allison Krause,
was the bullet
                        that blasted the flower.
Let every apple orchard blossom black,
                        black in mourning.
Ah, how the lilac smells!
                        You're without feeling.
Nothing. The President said it:
                        'You're a bum.'
All the dead are bums.
                        It's not their crime.
You lie in the grass,

17

                a melting candy in your mouth,
done with dressing in new clothes,
                            done with books.
You used to be a student.
                        You studied fine arts.
But other arts exist,
                of blood and terror,
and headsmen with a genius for the axe.
Who was Hitler?
                        A cubist of gas chambers.
In the name of all flowers
                    I curse your works,
you architects of lies,
                    maestros of murder!
Mothers of the world whisper
                        'O God, God'
and seers are afraid
            to look ahead.
Death dances rock-and-roll upon the bones
                            of Vietnam, Cambodia—
On what stage is it booked to dance tomorrow?
Rise up, Tokyo girls,
                    Roman boys,
take up your flowers
                against the common foe.
Blow the world's dandelions up
                        into a blizzard!
Flowers, to war!
                    Punish the punishers!
Tulip after tulip,
            carnation after carnation,
rip out of your tidy beds in anger,
choke every lying throat
                    with earth and root!
You, jasmine, clog
                the spinning blades of mine-layers!
Boldly,
        block the cross-hair sights,
        drive your sting into the lenses,
                            nettles!
Rise up, lily of the Ganges,

18

                lotus of the Nile,
stop the roaring props
            of planes pregnant
            with the death of children!
Roses, don't be proud
        to find yourselves sold
        at higher prices.
Nice as it is to touch a tender cheek,
thrust a sharper thorn a little deeper
                    into the fuel tanks of bombers.
Of course:
            Bullets are stronger than flowers.
Flowers aren't enough to overwhelm them.
Stems are too fragile,
                    petals are poor armor.
But a Vietnam girl of Allison's age,
                    taking a gun in her hands,
is the armed flower
                of the people's wrath!
If even flowers rise,
        then we've had enough
        of playing games with history.
Young America,
        tie up the killer's hands.
Let there be an escalation of truth
to overwhelm the escalating lie
                    crushing people's lives!
Flowers, make war!
            Defend what's beautiful!
Drown the city streets and country roads
                like the flood of an army advancing
and in the ranks of people and flowers
        arise, murdered Allison Krause,
Immortal of the age,
                Thorn-Flower of protest!

AN EXTRACT FROM:

THE FIRST THIRD

Neal Cassady

Chapter 1

For a time I held a unique position. Among the hundreds of
isolated creatures who haunted the streets of lower downtown
Denver there was not one so young as myself. Of these dreary
men who had committed themselves, each for his own good
reason, to the task of finishing their days as penniless drunkards,
I alone, as the sharer of their way of life, presented a replica of
childhood to which their vision could daily turn, and in being
thus grafted onto them, I became the unnatural son of a few
score beaten men.

It was my experience to be constantly meeting new cronies of
my father who invariably introduced me with a proud, 'This is
my boy.' Whereupon the pat on my head was usually followed
by the quizzical look the eye reserves for uncertainty, which here
conveyed the question, 'Shall I give him a little drink?' Sensing
the offer, backed by a half-extended bottle, my father would
always say, 'You'll have to ask him,' and I would coyly answer,
'No thank you, sir.' Of course this occurred only on those
memorable occasions when an acceptable drink like wine was
available. The unhappy times when there was none, with only
denatured alcohol (canned heat) or bay rum at hand, I did not
have to go through my little routine.

Many times, after normal adult catering with questions to
show interest in the child (such gestures of talkative comradeship
was their token parenthood, for these secondary fathers had

little else to give), I would be ignored while the talk of my father and his new friend turned to recalling the past. These tête-à-têtes were full of little asides which carried with them facts establishing that much of the life they had known was in common; their mutual type friends, cities visited, things done there, and so on. Their conversation had many general statements about Truth and Life, which contained the collective intelligence of all America's bums. They were drunkards whose minds, weakened by liquor and an obsequious manner of existence, seemed continually pre-occupied with bringing up short observations of obvious trash, said in such a way as to be instantly recognizable by the listener, who had heard it all before and whose own prime concern was to nod at everything said, then continue the conversation with a remark of his own, equally transparent and loaded with generalities. The simplicity of this pattern was marvellous and there was no limit to what they could agree on in this fashion and the abstract ends that could be reached. Through sheer repetitious hearing of such small-talk speculation, I came to know their minds so intimately that I could understand as they understood, and there was soon no mystery to the conversation of any of them. I assumed all men thought the same and so knew *these* things, because like any child I correlated all adult action without much actual regard for actual type.

All his fellow alcoholics called my father 'the barber' since he was 'bout the only one of them who had practised that trade and I was 'the barber's boy.' They all said I looked just like him but I didn't think this was true in the least. And they watched me grow with comments like 'Why, look there – his head is higher than your belt already!' It wasn't such a feat, I thought, to stand that tall, because my father had awfully short legs.

When, in 1932, the family situation was resolved by my parents' parting, I was not sorry to accompany my father in his retreat to Larimer Street. Most especially I was not sorry to bid what proved to be a two-year farewell to my terrifying bully-brother, Jimmy, and even to my less-thought-about mother and younger sister. The prospect of adventure filled my six-year-old head; besides, I would now be spared the sight of violence every Sunday. With my father gone for good, my older half-brothers Jack and Ralph would not be able to pound his face bloody when he returned so obediently home from his Saturday-night binges. Mother used to cry and beg them to stop beating him, but, as I observed many times in the years to follow, when these boys started using their fists there was only exhaustion to stop their brain-blinding rages.

But now all this and other such terrors, as when Jimmy made me fight other little boys, were behind me, and for the present I took an increased interest in my new surroundings so singularly uncommon and giving me so matchless an edification in observing the 'scum' right from the start. And I was given certain unorthodox freedoms not ordinarily to be had by American boys of six. My father, being usually drunk, or trying to get that way, was of necessity a bit lax in his discipline. Still, I didn't much take advantage of him, since I really loved the old boy.

It was the month of my sixth birthday and a usual fierce winter was upon the city when Dad and I moved into the Metropolitan. This was a five story building, condemned before I got there (though still not torn down 'til very recently) on the corner of 16th and Market Streets. In peril of collapse, it housed about a hundred of Denver's non-transient bums. On each of the upper floors there were some thirty-odd cubicles whose walls, failing by several feet to reach it, made the ceiling seem incongruously high. These sleeping cells mostly rented for ten or fifteen cents a night; certain superior ones cost two-bits, and we had one of these but only paid a weekly rate of one dollar since we shared the room with a third person.

This roommate of ours slept on a sort of platform made by a plank covering a pipe elbow in the building's plumbing. Not just anyone could sleep there in comfort, for the ledge was only about three feet long. But he fitted in the space snugly enough because both his legs had been amputated at the thigh many years ago. Appropriately, he was called Shorty and this fitting of name to fact seemed very funny to me. Every morning he got up early and, with his oversized arms, swung a skinny torso down those five flights of stairs. I never saw him pause to use the community washroom on the second floor, and presumed the sinks were too high for him so that he made toilet arrangements elsewhere. On the sidewalk he would get into a dolly-like cart and, using blocks of wood in each hand, push himself to his begging post. He usually went around the corner on Larimer Street and stationed himself before the Manhattan Restaurant. Larimer Street was Denver's main drag in the nineteenth century and the Manhattan was its best restaurant. Now everything else has fallen to cheapness but the fine Manhattan is still frequented by tourists and the well-to-do. Shorty's schedule was a few hours ahead of the bums with a normal length to their limbs, and he would often panhandle a dollar or more before noon because he had utilized his handicap by displaying it in this good spot. After he had gotten the price of a bottle or two, he would return to the room and drink into a stupor.

Usually he had passed out, or was about to, by the time I got home from school, but some days were slack, and on these days he would stay out very late. It was as though he had an early afternoon deadline, and if he wasn't in the room by then he wouldn't come at all. I came to dread these times because he would then drink on the street, and it was up to me to help search the alleys and doorways until we found him. Dad would carry him home while I followed, alternately pulling up hill and coasting down on his cart with the roller-skate wheels.

Now and again when, with child-energy, I burst into the room, I would catch Shorty playing with himself. (I thought it fried eggs littering the floor.) Even though he was past forty, any preoccupation with this form of diversion was justified, I'm sure. Judging from his appearance, he must not have had a woman since his youth, if then. Encrusted with dirt, he stank and was very ugly with a no-forehead face full of a grinning rubber mouth that showed black stubbed teeth. Yet his taste certainly did not run to boys my age, because the time or two I saw him exposed, he roared at me to get out, and these were the only instances of his anger that I recall.

My father and I lived with Shorty until June. After these four or five months, although I looked for him out of curiosity, we never saw him again. . . .

Perhaps the most exciting part of the day was the Metropolitan nights. Around the spacious main floor lobby were indiscriminately arranged numerous roundbacked chairs that supported with old wood squeakings of protest their pounds of weary flesh. Into this drafty high vaulted parlor of affliction crowded those dregs who had nothing to do and spent dreary hours of heavy time just sitting. But none sat in a position very near the pot-bellied stove in the rough floor's metal covered center, for, in contrast with the non-heated upper floors and the extreme cold outside, unwelcome waves of too much heat radiated from cherry colored cheeks of the overstoked stove, with its fiercely roaring always-open draft.

There was an inner lobby of smaller dimensions that was altogether more comfortable and unlike the outer lobby with its huge dirt-caked windows on which was advertised the price of beds. This room, except for a narrow door, had no break whatsoever in the filthy walls. In its confines there existed a pleasant intimacy quite missing in the foyer, because clustered about its tables were moneyless men killing time at cards. A year or two later, when the Metropolitan became even more overstuffed with society's sediments, the landlords (executors of a deceased plumber and pipefitter's large estate that had tinily begun in shrewd realty deals) removed what furniture filled this secondary lobby and put in cots to make a dormitory for the 'one-nighters'. But now, there was a continual round of knock-rummy, cribbage, Coon-Can, Casino, Pieute, Pinochle, Poker and other varieties of cardplaying. Here I spent much of the night learning to play most of the games fairly well, besides several slick card tricks in which I particularly delighted. I also passed many evening hours tossing my laboriously-made dart; it was a sewing needle inserted in a wooden match, the top of which was split to receive its feathers of newspaper that were held in place by thread. Despite my poor child-construction this contraption would work fine for the short time it went unstepped on. Of course, the unsturdy needle needed constant realigning and especially often must I re-crease the paper rotary blades so necessary for a balanced flight. Nevertheless, I loved my fragile weapon as I made it sail to the mark with throws of erratic southpaw speed. Without letup, save for the moments of adjustment, I ran back and forth between disgruntled onlookers, loosing the dart at everything stickable. All about the roomful of sitting men were these targets; a particular spot of scum in the wall plaster above their heads, a crack in the wooden floor, an empty chair, a window sill.

To the rear of the lobby, just to one side of the dark stairway opening, the dim golden color was still to be seen on grillwork of a cashier's cage. It was furnished with typical high-legged stool and black safe, reflecting from its dull finish the light of a tiny bulb aimed upon the dial combinations. In this small office domain sat the man who every night collected the pennies of incoming lodgers' rent. As they paid, each tenant scrawled his name and hometown on an ancient ledger book. When I had exhausted myself with darts and cards, it was my quiet pleasure to take this on my lap to scan its hundreds of ink-blotched pages.

It became my custom to curiously examine in regular private ritual all legible signatures and pronounce them to myself, to guess by their sound which names were aliases. Beginning with dates before my birth, the book of names of long-departed guests filled my mind with fascination. I became engrossed reading the long columns listing towns and states, comparing them geographically on the huge map, and particularly did I wonder at the different surnames and their origins; *all unknown to me each man's destiny and in daydreams imagining the variety of their possible fates I first consciously amazed at life.*

LAST NIGHT I DROVE A CAR

Gregory Corso

Last night I drove a car
    not knowing how to drive
    not owning a car
I drove and knocked down
    people I loved
    . . . went 120 through one town.

I stopped at Hedgeville
    and slept in the back seat
    . . . excited about my new life.

THE FOG

Miroslav Holub

The last path has fallen.
In the expiring fields round about
the victorious sea approaches
rocking on its waves
the voices of finches
and the voices of towns.

We are very far
out of both space and time,
we meet the crazy silhouettes
of wandering dinosaurs
and the radiated shadows of Martians
who cannot see for fear.

You wish to say something but
I don't understand:
between us lies
the immense corpse of reality
and out of its severed head
clotted white blood
comes billowing.

THE WRECK OF THE NORDLING

Gregory Corso

One night fifty men swam away from God
And drowned.
In the morning the abandoned God
Dipped His finger into the sea,
Came up with fifty souls,
And pointed towards eternity.

GOYA

Andrei Voznesensky

I am Goya: my eyes are destroyed
by enemy beaks.
Shell-holes stare from the naked field.

I am misery,

the Voice of War
the voice of charred cities' timber
on the snow of the Year
Forty-one.

I am the old woman's throat
who was hung, whose body sang like a bell
over the naked townsquare. . . .

I am Goya.
Grapes of Wrath! Dust
I am, raised by the barrage in the West.
Dust of the intruder. . . .

And bright stars
were hammered in the memorial sky

like nails.

Yes, I
am Goya.

English Version by
Anselm Hollo

MAD SONNET

Michael McClure

ON COLD SATURDAY I WALKED IN THE EMPTY
VALLEY OF WALL STREET
I dreamed with the hanging concrete eagles
and spoke with the black bronze foot of Washington.
I strode in the vibrations
of money-strength
in the narrow, cold, lovely CHASM.

*

Oh perfect chill slot of space!

WALL STREET, WALL STREET,
MOUNTED WITH DEAD BEASTS AND MEN
and metal placards greened and darkened.
And a cathedral at your head!

*

I see that the men are alive and born
and inspired
by the moving beauty of their own physical figures
who will tear
the vibrations-of-strength from the vibrations-of-money
and drop them like a dollar on the chests
of the Senate!
They step with the pride of a continent.

AN EXTRACT FROM:

THE WHITE NEGRO

Superficial Reflections on the Hipster

Norman Mailer

Our search for the rebels of the generation led us to the hipster. The hipster is an enfant terrible *turned inside out. In character with his time, he is trying to get back at the conformists by lying low. . . . You can't interview a hipster because his main goal is to keep out of society which, he thinks, is trying to make everyone over in its own image. He takes marijuana because it supplies him with experiences that can't be shared with 'squares'. He may affect a broad-brimmed hat or a zoot suit, but usually he prefers to skulk unmarked. The hipster may be a jazz musician; he is rarely an artist, almost never a writer. He may earn his living as a petty criminal, a hobo, a carnival roustabout or a free-lance moving man in Greenwich Village, but some hipsters have found a safe refuge in the upper income brackets as televison comics or movie actors. (The late James Dean, for one, was a hipster hero.) . . . It is tempting to describe the hipster in psychiatric terms as infantile, but the style of his infantilism is a sign of the times. He does not try to enforce his will on others, Napoleon-fashion, but contents himself with a magical omnipotence never disproved because never tested. . . . As the only extreme nonconformist of his generation, he exercises a powerful if underground appeal for conformists, through newspaper accounts of his delinquencies, his structureless jazz, and his emotive grunt words.*
–'Born 1930: The Unlost Generation' by Caroline Bird
Harper's Bazaar, Feb. 1957

Probably, we will never be able to determine the psychic havoc of the concentration camps and the atom bomb upon the unconscious mind of almost everyone alive in these years. For the first time in civilized history, perhaps for the first time in all of history, we have been forced to live with the suppressed knowledge that the smallest facets of our personality or the most minor projection of our ideas, or indeed the absence of ideas and the absence of personality could mean equally well that we might still be doomed to die as a cipher in some vast statistical operation in which our teeth would be counted, and our hair would be saved, but our death itself would be unknown, unhonored, and unremarked, a death which could not follow with dignity as a possible consequence to serious actions we had chosen, but rather a death by *deus ex machina* in a gas chamber or a radioactive city; and so if in the midst of civilization – that civilization founded upon the Faustian urge to dominate nature by mastering time, mastering the links of social cause and effect – in the middle of an economic civilization founded upon the confidence that time could indeed be subjected to our will, our psyche was subjected itself to the intolerable anxiety that death being causeless, life was causeless as well, and time deprived of cause and effect had come to a stop.

The Second World War presented a mirror to the human condition which blinded anyone who looked into it. For if tens of millions were killed in concentration camps out of the inexorable agonies and contractions of super-states founded upon the always insoluble contradictions of injustice, one was then obliged also to see that no matter how crippled and perverted an image of man was the society he had created, it was nonetheless his creation, his collective creation (at least his collective creation from the past) and if society was so murderous, then who could ignore the most hideous of questions about his own nature?

Worse. One could hardly maintain the courage to be individual, to speak with one's own voice, for the years in which one could complacently accept oneself as part of an elite by being a radical were forever gone. A man knew that when he dissented, he gave a note upon his life which could be called in any year of overt crisis. No wonder then that these have been the years of conform-

32

ity and depression. A stench of fear has come out of every pore of American life, and we suffer from a collective failure of nerve. The only courage, with rare exceptions, that we have been witness to, has been the isolated courage of isolated people.

II

It is on this bleak scene that a phenomenon has appeared: the American existentialist – the hipster, the man who knows that if our collective condition is to live with instant death by atomic war, relatively quick death by the State as *l'univers concentrationnaire*, or with a slow death by conformity with every creative and rebellious instinct stifled (at what damage to the mind and the heart and the liver and the nerves no research foundation for cancer will discover in a hurry), if the fate of twentieth century man is to live with death from adolescence to premature senescence, why then the only life-giving answer is to accept the terms of death, to live with death as immediate danger, to divorce oneself from society, to exist without roots, to set out on that uncharted journey into the rebellious imperatives of the self. In short, whether the life is criminal or not, the decision is to encourage the psychopath in oneself, to explore that domain of experience where security is boredom and therefore sickness, and one exists in the present, in that enormous present which is without past or future, memory or planned intention, the life where a man must go until he is beat, where he must gamble with his energies through all those small or large crises of courage and unforeseen situations which beset his day, where he must be with it or doomed not to swing. The unstated essence of Hip, its psychopathic brilliance, quivers with the knowledge that new kinds of victories increase one's power for new kinds of perception; and defeats, the wrong kind of defeats, attack the body and imprison one's energy until one is jailed in the prison air of other people's habits, other people's defeats, boredom, quiet desperation, and muted icy self-destroying rage. One is Hip or one is Square (the alternative which each new generation coming into American life is beginning to feel), one is a rebel or one conforms, one is a frontiersman in the Wild West of American night life, or else a Square cell, trapped in the totalitarian tissues of American society, doomed willy-nilly to conform if one is to succeed.

33

A totalitarian society makes enormous demands on the courage of men, and a partially totalitarian society makes even greater demands for the general anxiety is greater. Indeed if one is to be a man, almost any kind of unconventional action often takes disproportionate courage. So it is no accident that the source of Hip is the Negro for he has been living on the margin between totalitarianism and democracy for two centuries. But the presence of Hip as a working philosophy in the sub-words of American life is probably due to jazz, and its knife-like entrance into culture, its subtle but so penetrating influence on an avant-garde generation – that post-war generation of adventurers who (some consciously, some by osmosis) had absorbed the lessons of disillusionment and disgust of the Twenties, the Depression, and the War. Sharing a collective disbelief in the words of men who had too much money and controlled too many things, they knew almost as powerful a disbelief in the socially monolithic ideas of the single mate, the solid family and the respectable love life. If the intellectual antecedents of this generation can be traced to such separate influences as D. H. Lawrence, Henry Miller, and Wilhelm Reich, the viable philosophy of Hemingway fits most of their facts: in a bad world, as he was to say over and over again (while taking time out from his parvenu snobbery and dedicated gourmandise), in a bad world there is no love nor mercy nor charity nor justice unless a man can keep his courage, and this indeed fitted some of the facts. What fitted the need of the adventurer even more precisely was Hemingway's categorical imperative that what made him feel good became therefore The Good.

So no wonder that in certain cities of America, in New York of course, and New Orleans, in Chicago and San Francisco and Los Angeles, in such American cities as Paris and Mexico, D.F., this particular part of a generation was attracted to what the Negro had to offer. In such places as Greenwich Village, a ménage-a-trois was completed – the bohemian and the juvenile delinquent came face-to-face with the Negro, and the hipster was a fact in American life. If marijuana was the wedding ring, the child was the language of Hip for its argot gave expression to abstract states of feeling which all could share, at least all who were Hip. And in this wedding of the white and the black it was the Negro who brought the cultural dowry. Any Negro who wishes to live must live with danger from his first day, and no experience can

34

ever be casual to him, no Negro can saunter down a street with any real certainty that violence will not visit him on his walk. The cameos of security for the average white: mother and the home, job and the family, are not even a mockery to millions of Negroes; they are impossible. The Negro has the simplest of alternatives: live a life of constant humility or ever-threatening danger. In such a pass where paranoia is a vital to survival as blood, the Negro had stayed alive and begun to grow by following the need of his body where he could. Knowing in the cells of his existence that life was war, nothing but war, the Negro (all exceptions admitted) could rarely afford the sophisticated inhibitions of civilization, and so he kept for his survival the art of the primitive, he lived in the enormous present, he subsisted for his Saturday night kicks, relinquishing the pleasures of the body, and in his music he gave voice to the character and quality of his existence, to his rage and the infinite variations of joy, lust, languor, growl, cramp, pinch, scream and despair of his orgasm. For jazz is orgasm, it is the music of orgasm, good orgasm and bad, and so it spoke across a nation, it had the communication of art even where it was watered, perverted, corrupted, and almost killed, it spoke in no matter what laundered popular way of instantaneous existential states to which some whites could respond, it was indeed a communication by art because it said, 'I feel this, and now you do too'.

So there was a new breed of adventurers, urban adventurers who drifted out at night looking for action with a black man's code to fit their facts. The hipster had absorbed the existentialist synapses of the Negro, and for practical purposes could be considered a white Negro.

To be an existentialist, one must be able to feel oneself – one must know one's desires, one's rages, one's anguish, one must be aware of the character of one's frustration and know what would satisfy it. The over-civilised man can be an existentialist only if it is chic, and deserts it quickly for the next chic. To be a real existentialist (Sartre admittedly to the contrary) one must be religious, one must have one's sense of the 'purpose' – whatever the purpose may be – but a life which is directed by one's faith in the necessity of action is a life committed to the notion that the substratum of existence is the search, the end meaningful but mysterious; it is impossible to live such a life unless one's emotions provide their profound conviction. Only the French, alienated beyond alienation from their unconscious could welcome an existential philosophy without ever feeling it at all; indeed only a Frenchman by declaring that the unconscious did not exist could then proceed to explore the delicate involutions of consciousness, the microscopically sensuous and all but ineffable *frissons* of mental becoming, in order finally to create the theology of atheism and so submit that in a world of absurdities the existential absurdity is most coherent.

In the dialogue between the atheist and the mystic, the atheist is on the side of life, rational life, undialectical life – since he conceives of death as emptiness, he can, no matter how weary or despairing, wish for nothing but more life; his pride is that he does not transpose his weakness and spiritual fatigue into a romantic longing for death, for such appreciation of death is then all too capable of being elaborated by his imagination into a universe of meaningful structure and moral orchestration.

Yet this masculine argument can mean very little for the mystic. The mystic can accept the atheist's description of his weakness, he can agree that his mysticism was a response to despair. And yet . . . and yet his argument is that he, the mystic, is the one finally who has chosen to live with death, and so death is his experience and not the atheist's, and the atheist by eschewing the limitless dimensions of profound despair has rendered himself incapable to judge the experience. The real argument which the mystic must always advance is the very intensity of his private vision – his argument depends from the vision precisely because what was felt in the vision is so extraordinary that no rational argument, no hypotheses of 'oceanic feelings' and certainly no skeptical reductions can explain away what has become for him the reality more real than the reality of closely reasoned logic. His inner experience of the possibilities within death is his logic. So, too, for the existentialist. And the psychopath. And the saint and the bullfighter and the lover. The common denominator for all of them is their burning consciousness of the present, exactly that incandescent consciousness which the possibilities within death has opened for them. There is a depth of desperation to the condition which enables one to remain in life only by engaging death, but the reward is their knowledge that what is happening at each instant of the electric present is good or bad for them, good or bad for their cause, their love, their action, their need.

It is this knowledge which provides the curious community of feeling in the world of the hipster, a muted cool religious revival to be sure, but the element which is exciting, disturbing, nightmarish perhaps, is that incompatibles have come to bed, the inner life and the violent life, the orgy and the dream of love, the desire to murder and the desire to create, a dialectical conception of existence with a lust for power, a dark, romantic, and yet undeniably dynamic view of existence for it sees every man and woman as moving individually through each moment of life forward into growth or backward into death.

TO HARPO MARX

Jack Kerouac

O Harpo! When did you seem like an angel
    the last time?
    and played the gray harp of gold?

When did you steal the silverware
    and bug-spray the guests?

When did your brother find rain
    in your sunny courtyard?

When did you chase your last blonde
    across the Millionairesses' lawn
    with a bait hook on a line
    protruding from your bicycle?

Or when last you powderpuffed
    your white flour face
    with fishbarrel cover?

Harpo! Who was that Lion
    I saw you with?

How did you treat the midget
    and Konk the giant?

Harpo, in your recent night-club appearance
    in New Orleans were you old?
    Were you still chiding with your horn
    in the cane at your golden belt?

Did you still emerge from your pockets
  another Harpo, or screw on
  new wrists?

Was your vow of silence an Indian Harp?

1959

DEMENTIA IN AN AFRICAN APARTMENT HOUSE

Gregory Corso

A bullet-holed lion excited the dying child
    by yelping two-legged across the floor
    by scratching two-legged upon the door
The witch-doctor plugged his ears – the mother went wild!
Lion blood trailed the white sheets paw by paw.

The father came home the following year
    threw a week's purse with a curse
    into the witch-doctor's lap that couldn't hear
The wife sat in a corner scrubbing the skin of the lion.

'Make the bed! Make the bed!' he said.

She took the lion to another room
Came back; washed the blood from the door,
    put the dead child on the floor
And cleaned the sheets with a broom.

That night as the father lay sleeping
The wounded lion came in creeping;
The wife ran up to it, and on her knees fell:
'Lion, lion,' she said, 'my mind is not well.'

Mayakovsky's

SUICIDE NOTE

She loves me, loves me not.
                        I tear my fingers
and scatter them,
              broken,
as one tears
              superstitiously
                        scattering all over May
the little daisy wreath.
Let the haircut and close shave
                    reveal
                        greyness,
the silver of years
              pound.
I hope,
        I believe:
              I never shall be
one
     of shameful prudence.
It's two o'clock already.
                    I guess you're in bed.
The Milky Way
             a silver river
                  in the night.
I'm in no hurry,
            there's no point
waking
        troubling you
              with telegrams.
Like they say,

the incident is closed.
The loveboat simply
cracked up against circumstance.
You and I,
quits,
and no use listing
mutual griefs,
miseries,
hurts.
Look at how quiet
the world is.
Night
has levied a tax
of stars in the sky.
In such moments
one gets up
and speaks to
ages,
history,
the whole cosmos.
It's two o'clock . . .
I guess you're in bed.
Or maybe you're
also up with this thing.
I'm in no hurry.
There's no point
waking
troubling you
with telegrams.

—translated by Victor Erlich & Jack Hirschman.

COAT OF ARMS

Philip Lamantia

Pure as gale and mist washing my skull
pure as silk dances on the ocean's knee
  thong thighs of the walking coast
pure as Mendocino witch havens
  through the transparent plumes of extinct birds
looking down from the sky-people boat
exploding over candy castles
  the salt wisdom pervades
safe as the mummy's purity *is* from the congresses of fear

The night goes up
into the ventricles of King Novalis
and horned men descend the saline stairway
whose bones are lit up from astral lamps
of the great genii, Ignis phana, pure claw
that brushes death's meat
awakened without a body on the edge of the clubfooted wave

Going around blind corners, the sylph
breaks her teeth on the borders of three continents
I pass without passports –
rapid vision overtakes the storm
of this glittering void I love
and reveals everything in a speeding cloud!

This is the moral for inventing ecstasies
Freed from the clutch of memory
I eat the eagle's windy branches
  my eye the lion's cave

silver fluids fix my voice
that sings *The World and I Are One!*
What's newly hatched is born from dying seed!

To let loose a room's inner skeleton
I come from far places
dressed in the explosions of green lamps
It's the moment before arson
Taught not to look back
my fires drink a porous stone
   The geyser speaks
   at the house of the onyx mirror
   My name is augur
   these lips besmirch the dawn
   My sword's a vaporous cloud
The tooth marks of ecstasy
wear the look of totems
and the dragon's vermouth tongue
Every arm is bathed in silver blood
   I read the spells of Egypt patiently

9.1.59: II

Pablo Picasso

then the mailman came and
the collector of handclapping and olés
and the parish blindman
and the blackbird
Ramon's daughters and doña Paquita's also
the oldest daughter   the old maid
and the priest standing coldly apart painted
saffron and green
loaded with noodles and black
grapes of cotton and aloes   fat and
very erect   become radishes and
fryingpan full of eggs
and home fries   fried
cracklings covered with fleas
and cattle bells and the question
carried on the shoulder   poor
and rich swept off by the rainstorm
above the burning wheat   soaking
his shirt with
hail   the dirty linen

I AM DYING, MEESTER?

William Burroughs

Panama clung to our bodies – Probably cut – Anything made this dream – It has consumed the customers of fossil orgasm – Ran into my old friend Jones – So badly off, forgotten, coughing in 1920 movie – Vaudeville voices hustle sick dawn breath on bed service – Idiot Mambo spattered backwards – I nearly suffocated trying on the boy's breath – That's Panama – Nitrous flesh swept out by your voice and end of receiving set – Brain eating birds patrol the low frequency brain waves – Post card waiting forgotten civilians 'and they are all on jelly fish, Meester – Panama photo town – Dead post card of junk.'

Sad hand down backward time track – Genital pawn ticket peeled his stale underwear – Brief boy on screen laughing my skivies all the way down – Whispers of dark street in Puerto Assis – Meester smiles through the village wastrel – Orgasm siphoned back telegram: 'Johnny pants down.' – (That stale summer dawn smell in the garage – Vines twisting through steel – Bare feet in dog's excrement.)

Panama clung to our bodies from Las Palmas to David on camphor sweet smells of cooking paregoric – Burned down the republic – The druggist no glot clom Fliday – Panama mirrors of 1910 under seal in any drug store – He threw in the towel, morning light on cold coffee –

Junk kept nagging me: 'Lushed in East St Louis, I knew you'd come scraping bone – Once a junky always spongy and rotten – I knew your life – Junk sick four days there.'

Stale breakfast table – Little cat smile – Pain and death smell of his sickness in the room with me – Three souvenir shots of Panama city – Old friend came and stayed all day – Face eaten by 'I need more' – I have noticed this in the New World – 'You

46

come with me, Meester?'

And Joselito moved in at Las Playas during the essentials –
Stuck in this place – Iridescent lagoons, swamp delta, gas flares –
Bubbles of coal gas still be saying 'A ver, Luckees!' a hundred
years from now – A rotting teak wood balcony propped up by
Ecuador.

'The brujo began crooning a special case – It was like going
under ether into the eyes of a shrunken head – Numb, covered
with layers of cotton – Don't know if you got my last hints
trying to break out of this numb dizziness with Chinese characters
– All I want is out of here – Hurry up please – Took possession of
me – How many plots have made a botanical expedition like
this before they could take place? – Scenic railways – I am dying
cross wine dizziness – I was saying over and over 'shifted com-
missions where the awning flaps' Flashes in front of my eyes
your voice and end of the line.'

That whinning Panama clung to our bodies – I went into
Chico's Bar on mouldy pawn ticket, waiting in 1920 movie for
a rum coke – Nitrous flesh under this honky tonk swept out by
your voice: 'Driving Nails In My Coffin' – Brain eating birds
patrol 'Your Cheating Heart' – Dead post card waiting a place
forgotten – Light concussion of 1920 movie – Casual adolescent
had undergone special G.I. processing – Evening on the boy's
flesh naked – Kept trying to touch in sleep – 'Old photographer
trick wait for Johnny – Here goes Mexican cemetery.' On the
sea wall met a boy with red and white striped T shirt – P.G. town
in the purple twilight – The boy pealed off his stale underwear
scraping erection – Warm rain on the iron roof – Under the
ceiling fan stood naked on bed service – Bodies touched electric
film, contact sparks tingled – Fan whiffs of young hard on
washing adolescent T shirt – The blood smells drowned voices
and end of the line – That's Panama – Sad movie drifting in
islands of rubbish, black lagoons and fish people waiting a
place forgotten – Fossil honky tonk swept out by a ceiling fan –
Old photographer trick tuned them out.

'I am dying, Meester?'

Flashes in front of my eyes naked and sullen – Rotten dawn
wind in sleep – Death rot on Panama photo where the awning
flaps.

47

IN BACK OF THE REAL

Allen Ginsberg

railroad yard in San Jose
    I wandered desolate
in front of a tank factory
    and sat on a bench
near the switchman's shack.

A flower lay on the hay on
    the asphalt highway
– the dread hay flower
    I thought – It had a
brittle black stem and
    corolla of yellowish dirty
spikes like Jesus' inchlong
    crown, and a soiled
dry center cotton tuft
    like a used shaving brush
that's been lying under
    the garage for a year.

Yellow, yellow flower, and
    flower of industry,
tough spikey ugly flower,
    flower nonetheless,
with the form of the great yellow
    Rose in your brain!
This is the flower of the World.

THE LAST WARMTH
OF ARNOLD

Gregory Corso

Arnold, warm with God,
hides beneath the porch
remembering the time of escape, imprisoned in Vermont,
shoveling snow. Arnold was from somewhere else,
where it was warm; where he wore suede shoes
and played ping-pong.
Arnold knew the Koran.
And he knew to sing:
    Young Julien Sorel
    Knew his Latin well
    And was wise as he
    Was beautiful
    Until his head fell.

In the empty atmosphere
Arnold kept a tiplet pigeon, a bag of chicken corn.
He thought of Eleanor, her hands;
watched her sit sad in school
He got Carmine to lure her into the warm atmosphere;
he wanted to kiss her, live with her forever;
break her head with bargains.

Who is Arnold? Well,
I first saw him wear a black cap
covered with old Wilkie buttons. He was 13.
And afraid. But with a smile. And he was always
willing to walk you home, to meet your mother,

49

to tell her about Hester Street Park
about the cold bums there;
about the cold old Jewish ladies who sat,
hands folded, sad, keeping their faces
away from the old Jewish Home.
Arnold grew up with a knowledge of bookies
and chicken pluckers.

And Arnold knew to sing:
    Dead now my 15th year
    F.D.R., whose smiling face
    Made evil the buck-toothed Imperialist,
    The moustached Aryan,
    The jut-jawed Caesar –
    Dead now, and I weep . . .
    For once I did hate that man
    and no reason
    but innocent hate
    – my cap decked with old Wilkie buttons.

Arnold was kicked in the balls
by an Italian girl who got mad
because there was a big coal strike on
and it forced the Educational Alliance to close its doors.
Arnold, weak and dying, stole pennies from the library,
but he also read about Paderewski.
He used to walk along South Street
wondering about the various kinds of glue.
And it was about airplane glue he was thinking
when he fell and died beneath the Brooklyn Bridge.

6

Lawrence Ferlinghetti

        And the Arabs asked terrible questions
and the Pope didn't know what to say and the people
ran around in wooden shoes asking which way was the
head of Midas facing and everyone said

        No instead of Yes

        While still forever in the Luxembourg
gardens in the fountains of the Medicis were the
  fat red goldfish and the fat white goldfish
    and the children running around the pool
      pointing and piping
                Des poissons rouges!
  Des poissons rouges!

              but they ran off
    and a leaf unhooked itself
              and fell upon the pool
    and lay like an eye winking
              circles
and then the pool was very

        still

           and there was a dog
     just standing there
           at the edge of the pool
       looking down
           at the tranced fish

51

and not barking
                or waving its funny tail or
                                    anything

        so that

                    for a moment then
        in the late November dusk

silence hung like a lost idea
                        and a statue turned

            its head

A QUESTIONNAIRE

Anselm Hollo

First question is do you enjoy fucking & we're not asking you
   whom or what plain yes or no will do.
Second if yes you want to go on doing it once in a while we're
   not asking you how frequently plain yes or no will do.
If not then what do you enjoy?
But if you yes want to go on at least once in a while or now &
   again do you believe they'll drop bombs on you to stop you.
And if you don't enjoy much anything don't you think you might
   as well die & if yes why don't you.
If yes to the other that is you believe the commies want to stop
   you eating drinking fucking or just walking about we suggest
   you go there & see for yourself.
If on the other hand you expect things to be going on much the
   same after all systems go & crunch you're obviously a caveman
   type & outside the scope of our inquiry.

IN THE EARLY MORNING

Gregory Corso

In the early morning
             beside the runaway hand-in-pocket
             whistling youth
I see the hopping drooling Desirer
His black legs . . . the corncob pipe and cane
The long greasy coat, and the bloodstained
        fingernails
He is waiting
             flat against the trees

URIAH HEEP

a London Poem

Yevgeny Yevtushenko

It's sad: but Mr Heep
ain't dead. Here he is, feebly grinning, rabbity eyes
an albino checking our passports
here he is, digging into our luggage
our shirts – the tins of caviar –
disappearing into the suitcase with huge wet ears
that seem to be growing longer all the time . . .
He's looking
for something, some kind of bonus.
Perhaps
the H-Bomb??
He can't find it. Says, 'Here you are' shrugging
drops out of our sight –
Forgive me, England
yes forgive me for starting my poem like this!
I met such great people there
yes really good people, I have to call them my own!
But still, but still
that creep Uriah Heep is still with us –
he must have holed up somewhere,
he's still around
cheering the neo-fascists, heap lot of good
that'll do him
writing weird articles in the Daily Mail
putting down everybody
who still isn't for sale.
Coming on strong about 'morals', all that.

Putting down Mr Pickwick,
really running poor Mr Pickwick into the ground.
Looking at me
as if he was going to sell me the Keys
of the Kingdom – sexless, creepy
he terrifies me!
I've heard people say, who come on like thinkers
that genius and creepiness
are immortal . . .
I dunno. Anyway, Heep, I think one day
we'll stand by your grave,
England and I,
much closer together under this sky!

London 1961

English Version by
Anselm Hollo

AN EXTRACT FROM:

ECO-CATASTROPHE

Dr Paul Ehrlich

In the following scenario, Dr Paul Ehrlich predicts what our world will be like in ten years if the present course of environmental destruction is allowed to continue. Dr Ehrlich is a prominent ecologist, a professor of biology at Stamford University, and author of The Population Bomb (*Ballantine*).

I

The end of the ocean came late in the summer of 1979, and it came even more rapidly than the biologists had expected. There had been signs for more than a decade, commencing with the discovery in 1968 that DDT slows down photosynthesis in marine plant life. It was announced in a short paper in the technical journal, Science, but to ecologists it smacked of doomsday. They knew that all life in the sea depends on photosynthesis, the chemical process by which green plants bind the sun's energy and make it available to living things. And they knew that DDT and similar chlorinated hydrocarbons had polluted the entire surface of the earth, including the sea.

But that was only the first of many signs. There had been the final gasp of the whaling industry in 1973, and the end of the Peruvian anchovy fishery in 1975. Indeed, a score of other fisheries had disappeared quietly from over-exploitation and various eco-catastrophes by 1977. The term 'eco-catastrophe' was coined by a California ecologist in 1969 to describe the most spectacular of man's attacks on the systems which sustain his life. He drew his inspiration from the Santa Barbara offshore oil disaster of that year, and from the news which spread among naturalists that virtually all of the Golden State's seashore bird life was doomed because of chlorinated hydrocarbon interference with its reproduction. Eco-catastrophes in the sea became increasingly common in the early 1970's. Mysterious 'blooms' of previously rare micro-organisms began to appear in offshore waters. Red tides – killer outbreaks of a minute single-celled plant – returned to the Florida Gulf coast and were sometimes accompanied by tides of other exotic hues.

It was clear by 1975 that the entire ecology of the ocean was changing. A few types of phytoplankton were becoming resistant to chlorinated hydrocarbons and were gaining the upper hand. Changes in the phytoplankton community led inevitably to changes in the community of zooplankton, the tiny animals which eat the phytoplankton. These changes were passed on up chains of life in the ocean to the herring, plaice, cod and tuna. As the diversity of life in the ocean diminished, its stability also decreased.

Other changes had taken place by 1975. Most ocean fishes that returned to fresh water to breed, like the salmon, had become extinct, their breeding streams so dammed up and polluted that their powerful homing instinct only resulted in suicide. Many fishes and shellfishes that bred in restricted areas along the coasts followed them as onshore pollution escalated.

By 1977 the annual yield of fish from the sea was down to 30 million metric tons, less than one-half the per capita catch of a decade earlier. This helped malnutrition to escalate sharply in a world where an estimated 50 million people per year were already dying of starvation. The United Nations attempted to get all chlorinated hydrocarbon insecticides banned on a world-wide basis, but the move was defeated by the United States. This opposition was generated primarily by the American petro-chemical industry, operating hand in glove with its subsidiary, the United States Department of Agriculture. Together they per-suaded the government to oppose the U.N. move – which was not difficult since most Americans believed that Russia and China were more in need of fish products than was the United States. The United Nations also attempted to get fishing nations to adopt strict and enforced catch limits to preserve dwindling stocks. This move was blocked by Russia, who, with the most modern electronic equipment, was in the best position to glean what was left in the sea. It was, curiously, on the very day in 1977 when the Soviet Union announced its refusal that another ominous article appeared in Science. It announced that incident solar radiation had been so reduced by worldwide air pollution that serious effects on the world's vegetation could be expected.

II

Apparently it was a combination of ecosystem destabilisation, sunlight reduction, and a rapid escalation in chlorinated hydrocarbon pollution from massive Thanodrin applications which triggered the ultimate catastrophe. Seventeen huge Soviet-financed Thanodrin plants were operating in underdeveloped countries by 1978. They had been part of a massive Russian 'aid offensive' designed to fill the gap caused by the collapse of America's ballyhooed 'Green Revolution.'

It became apparent in the early '70s that the 'Green Revolution' was more talk than substance. Distribution of high yield 'miracle' grain seeds had caused temporary local spurts in agricultural production. Simultaneously, excellent weather had produced record harvests. The combination permitted bureaucrats, especially in the United States Department of Agriculture and the Agency for International Development (AID), to reverse their previous pessimism and indulge in an outburst of optimistic propaganda about staving off famine. They raved about the approaching transformation of agriculture in the underdeveloped countries (UDCs). The reason for the propaganda reversal was never made clear. Most historians agree that a combination of utter ignorance of ecology, a desire to justify past errors, and pressure from agro-industry (which was eager to sell pesticides, fertilizers, and farm machinery to the UDCs and agencies helping the UDCs) was behind the campaign. Whatever the motivation, the results were clear. Many concerned people, lacking the expertise to see through the Green Revolution drivel, relaxed. The population-food crisis was 'solved'.

But reality was not long in showing itself. Local famine persisted in northern India even after good weather brought an end to the ghastly Bihar famine of the mid-'60s. East Pakistan was next, followed by a resurgence of general famine in northern India. Other foci of famine rapidly developed in Indonesia, the Philippines, Malawi, the Congo, Egypt, Colombia, Ecuador, Honduras, the Dominican Republic, and Mexico.

Everywhere hard realities destroyed the illusion of the Green Revolution. Yields dropped as the progressive farmers who had first accepted the new seeds found that their higher yields brought lower prices – effective demand (hunger plus cash) was not sufficient in poor countries to keep prices up. Less progressive farmers, observing this, refused to make the extra effort required to cultivate the 'miracle' grains. Transport systems proved inadequate to bring the necessary fertilizer to the fields where the new and extremely fertilizer-sensitive grains were being grown. The same systems were also inadequate to move produce to markets. Fertilizer plants were not built fast enough, and most of the underdeveloped countries could not scrape together funds to purchase supplies, even on concessional terms. Finally, the inevitable happened, and pests began to reduce yields in even the most carefully cultivated fields. Among the first were the famous 'miracle rats' which invaded Philippine 'miracle rice' fields early in 1969. They were quickly followed by many insects and viruses, thriving on the relatively pest-susceptible new grains, encouraged by the vast and dense plantings, and rapidly acquiring resistance to the chemicals used against them. As chaos spread until even the most obtuse agriculturists and economists realized that the Green Revolution had turned brown, the Russians stepped in.

In retrospect it seems incredible that the Russians, with the American mistakes known to them, could launch an even more incompetent program of aid to the underdeveloped world. Indeed, in the early 1970's there were cynics in the United States who claimed that outdoing the stupidity of American foreign aid would be physically impossible. Those critics were, however, obviously unaware that the Russians had been busily destroying their own environment for many years. The virtual disappearance of sturgeon from Russian rivers caused a great shortage of caviar by 1970. A standard joke among Russian scientists at that time was that they had created an artificial caviar which was indistinguishable from the real thing – except by taste. At any rate the Soviet Union, observing with interest the progressive deterioration of relations between the UDCs and the United States, came up with a solution. It had recently developed what it claimed was the ideal insecticide, a highly lethal chlorinated hydrocarbon complexed with a special agent for penetrating the external skeletal armor of insects. Announcing that the new pesticide, called Thanodrin, would truly produce a Green Revolution, the Soviets entered into negotiations with various UDCs for the construction of massive Thanodrin factories. The USSR would bear all the costs; all it wanted in return were certain trade and military concessions.

It is interesting now, with the perspective of years, to examine in some detail the reasons why the UDCs welcomed the Thanodrin plan with such open arms. Government officials in these countries ignored the protests of their own scientists that Thanodrin would not solve the problems which plagued them. The governments now knew that the basic cause of their problems was overpopulation, and that these problems had been exacerbated by the dullness, daydreaming, and cupidity endemic to all governments. They knew that only population control and limited development aimed primarily at agriculture could have spared them the horrors they now faced. They knew it, but they were not about to admit it. How much easier it was simply to accuse the Americans of failing to give them proper aid; how much simpler to accept the Russian panacea.

And then there was the general worsening of relations between the United States and the UDCs. Many things had contributed to this. The situation in America in the first half of the 1970's deserves our close scrutiny. Being more dependent on imports for raw materials than the Soviet Union, the United States had, in the early 1970's, adopted more and more heavy-handed policies in order to insure continuing supplies. Military adventures in Asia and Latin America had further lessened the international credibility of the United States as a great defender of freedom – an image which had begun to deteriorate rapidly during the pointless and fruitless Viet-Nam conflict. At home, acceptance of the carefully manufactured image lessened dramatically, as even the more romantic and chauvinistic citizens began to understand the role of the military and the industrial system in what John Kenneth Galbraith had aptly named 'The New Industrial State'.

At home in the USA the early '70s were traumatic times. Racial violence grew and the habitability of the cities diminished, as nothing substantial was done to ameliorate either racial inequities or urban blight. Welfare rolls grew as automation and general technological progress forced more and more people into the category of 'unemployable'. Simultaneously a taxpayers' revolt occurred. Although there was not enough money to build the schools, roads, water systems, sewage systems, jails, hospitals, urban transit lines, and all the other amenities needed to support a burgeoning population, Americans refused to tax themselves more heavily. Starting in Youngstown, Ohio in 1969 and followed closely by Richmond, California, community after community was forced to close its schools or curtail educational operations for lack of funds. Water supplies, already marginal in quality and quantity in many places by 1970, deteriorated quickly. Water rationing occurred in 1723 municipalities in the summer of 1974, and hepatitis and epidemic dysentery rates climbed about 500 per cent between 1970-1974.

III

Air pollution continued to be the most obvious manifestation of environmental deterioration. It was, by 1972, quite literally in the eyes of all Americans. The year 1973 saw not only the New York and Los Angeles smog disasters, but also the publication of the Surgeon General's massive report on air pollution and health. The public had been partially prepared for the worst by the publicity given to the U.N. pollution conference held in 1972. Deaths in the late '60s caused by smog were well known to scientists, but the public had ignored them because they mostly involved the early demise of the old and sick rather than people dropping dead on the freeways. But suddenly our citizens were faced with nearly 200,000 corpses and massive documentation that they could be the next to die from respiratory disease. They were not ready for that scale of disaster. After all, the U.N. conference had not predicted that accumulated air pollution would make the planet uninhabitable until amost 1990. The population was terrorized as TV screens became filled with scenes of horror from the disaster areas. Especially vivid was NBC's coverage of hundreds of unattended people choking out their lives outside of New York's hospitals. Terms like nitrogen oxide, acute bronchitis and cardiac arrest began to have real meaning for most Americans.

The ultimate horror was the announcement that chlorinated hydrocarbons were now a major constituent of air pollution in all American cities. Autopsies of smog disaster victims revealed an average chlorinated hydrocarbon load in fatty tissue equivalent to 26 parts per million of DDT. In October, 1973, the Department of Health, Education and Welfare announced studies which showed unequivocally that increasing death rates from hypertension, cirrhosis of the liver, liver cancer and a series of other diseases had resulted from the chlorinated hydrocarbon load. They estimated that Americans born since 1946 (when DDT usage began) now had a life expectancy of only 49 years, and predicted that if current patterns continued, this expectancy would reach 42 years by 1980, when it might level out. Plunging insurance stocks triggered a stock market panic. The president of Velsicol, Inc., a major pesticide producer, went on television to 'publicly eat a teaspoonful of DDT' (it was really powdered milk) and announce that HEW had been infiltrated by Communists. Other giants of the petro-chemical industry, attempting to dispute the indisputable evidence, launched a massive pressure campaign on Congress to force HEW to 'get out of agriculture's business'. They were aided by the agro-chemical journals, which had decades of experience in misleading the public about the benefits and dangers of pesticides. But by now the public realized that it had been duped. The Nobel Prize for medicine and physiology was given to Drs J. L. Radomski and W. B. Deichmann, who in the late 1960's had pioneered in the documentation of the long-term lethal effects of chlorinated hydrocarbons. A Presidential Commission with unimpeachable credentials directly accused the agro-chemical complex of 'condemning many millions of Americans to an early death'. The year 1973 was the year in which Americans finally came to understand the direct threat to their existence posed by environmental deterioration.

And 1973 was also the year in which most people finally comprehended the indirect threat. Even the president of Union Oil Company and several other industrialists publicly stated their concern over the reduction of bird populations which had resulted from pollution by DDT and other chlorinated hydrocarbons. Insect populations boomed because they were resistant to most pesticides and had been freed, by the incompetent use of those pesticides, from most of their natural enemies. Rodents swarmed over crops, multiplying rapidly in the absence of predatory birds. The effect of pests on the wheat crop was especially disastrous in the summer of 1973, since that was also the year of the great drought. Most of us can remember the shock which greeted the announcement by atmospheric physicists that the shift of the jet stream which had caused the drought was probably permanent. It signalled the birth of the Midwestern desert. Man's air-polluting activities had by then caused gross changes in climatic patterns. The news, of course, played hell with commodity and stock markets. Food prices skyrocketed, as savings were poured into hoarded canned goods. Official assurances that food supplies would remain ample fell on deaf ears, and even the government showed signs of nervousness when California migrant field workers went out on strike again in protest against the continued use of pesticides by growers. The strike burgeoned into farm burning and riots. The workers, calling themselves 'The Walking Dead', demanded immediate compensation for their shortened lives, and crash research programs to attempt to lengthen them.

It was in the same speech in which President Edward Kennedy, after much delay, finally declared a national emergency and called out the National Guard to harvest California's crops, that the first mention of population control was made. Kennedy pointed out that the United States would no longer be able to offer any food aid to other nations and was likely to suffer food shortages herself. He suggested that, in view of the manifest failure of the Green Revolution, the only hope of the UDCs lay in population control. His statement, you will recall, created an uproar in the underdeveloped countries. Newspaper editorials accused the United States of wishing to prevent small countries from becoming large nations and thus threatening American hegemony. Politicians asserted that President Kennedy was a 'creature of the giant drug combine' that wished to shove its pills down every woman's throat.

Among Americans, religious opposition to population control was very slight. Industry in general also backed the idea. Increasing poverty in the UDCs was both destroying markets and threatening supplies of raw materials. The seriousness of the raw material situation had been brought home during the Congressional Hard Resources hearings in 1971. The exposure of the ignorance of the cornucopian economists had been quite a spectacle – a spectacle brought into virtually every American's home in living color. Few would forget the distinguished geologist from the University of California who suggested that economists be legally required to learn at least the most elementary facts of geology. Fewer still would forget that an equally distinguished Harvard economist added that they might be required to learn some economics, too. The overall message was clear: America's resource situation was bad and bound to get worse. The hearings had led to a bill requiring the Departments of State, Interior, and Commerce to set up a joint resource procurement council with the express purpose of 'insuring that proper consideration of American resource needs be an integral part of American foreign policy'.

IV

Suddenly the United States discovered that it had a national consensus: population control was the only possible salvation of the underdeveloped world. But that same consensus led to heated debate. How could the UDCs be persuaded to limit their populations, and should not the United States lead the way by limiting its own? Members of the intellectual community wanted America to set an example. They pointed out that the United States was in the midst of a new baby boom: her birth rate, well over 20 per thousand per year, and her growth rate of over one per cent per annum were among the very highest of the developed countries. They detailed the deterioration of the American physical and psychic environments, the growing health threats, the impending food shortages, and the insufficiency of funds for desperately needed public works. They contended that the nation was clearly unable or unwilling to properly care for the people it already had. What possible reason could there be, they queried, for adding any more? Besides, who would listen to requests by the United States for population control when that nation did not control her own profligate reproduction?

Those who opposed population controls for the U.S. were equally vociferous. The military-industrial complex, with its all-too-human mixture of ignorance and avarice, still saw strength and prosperity in numbers. Baby food magnates, already worried by the growing nitrate pollution of their products, saw their market disappearing. Steel manufacturers saw a decrease in aggregate demand and slippage for that holy of holies, the Gross National Product. And military men saw, in the growing population-food-environment crisis, a serious threat to their carefully nurtured Cold War. In the end, of course, economic arguments held sway, and the 'inalienable right of every American couple to determine the size of its family', a freedom invented for the occasion in the early '70s, was not compromised.

The population control bill, which was passed by Congress early in 1974, was quite a document, nevertheless. On the domestic front, it authorized an increase from 100 to 150 million dollars in funds for 'family planning' activities. This was made possible by a general feeling in the country that the growing army on welfare needed family planning. But the gist of the bill was a series of measures designed to impress the need for population control on the UDCs. All American aid to countries with overpopulation problems was required by law to consist in part of population control assistance. In order to receive any assistance each nation was required not only to accept the population control aid, but also to match it according to a complex formula. 'Overpopulation' itself was defined by a formula based on U.N. statistics, and the UDCs were required not only to accept aid, but also to show progress in reducing birth rates. Every five years the status of the aid program for each nation was to be re-evaluated.

The reaction to the announcement of this program dwarfed the response to President Kennedy's speech. A coalition of UDCs attempted to get the U.N. General Assembly to condemn the United States as a 'genetic aggressor'. Most damaging of all to the American cause was the famous '25 Indians and a dog' speech by Mr Shankarnarayan, Indian Ambassador to the U.N. Shankarnarayan pointed out that for several decades the United States, with less than six per cent of the people of the world had consumed roughly 50 per cent of the raw materials used every year. He described vividly America's contribution to worldwide environmental deterioration, and he scathingly denounced the miserly record of United States foreign aid as 'unworthy of a fourth-rate power, let alone the most powerful nation on earth'.

It was the climax of his speech, however, which most historians claim once and for all destroyed the image of the United States.

Shankarnarayan informed the assembly that the average American family dog was fed more animal protein per week than the average Indian got in a month. 'How do you justify taking fish from protein-starved Peruvians and feeding them to your animals?' he asked. 'I contend', he concluded, 'that the birth of an American baby is a greater disaster for the world than that of 25 Indian babies.' When the applause had died away, Mr Sorensen, the American representative, made a speech which said essentially that 'other countries look after their own self-interest, too.' When the vote came, the United States was condemned.

BUT I WILL BE GONE

Semyon Kirsanov

But I will be gone
    beyond the horizon
and you will be gone
    beyond the horizon

    But you will be gone
beyond the horizon
    like the day –

But I will be gone
  beyond the horizon
    like the shadow
  is gone
    when the day is moving
away, across
            the dunes

*English Version by
Anselm Hollo*

9.1.59: IV

Pablo Picasso

when the mailman figured
out what the little girl was doing
on the brownish velvet cloth blue
from the flock of toads praying under
neath the black/an/blue turquoise the
piece of cloak stained coral from the rag
the ball of jasmine
to whistle up their
amphoras and their oxen
he did his silly acrobatics again
and ran afoul of the plot –
Nothing missing but the
arrival of the queen mother colonel
and her daughters
so that the function blew up in the hand
the girl got all tangled up in her calculations
and a seed jumped out and up her rump, not
to order or
by ordinance
as God ordains
nor by pharmaceutical recognition
certainly not
just to be pleasant

THE OWL

Philip Lamantia

I hear him, see him – interpenetrate
those shadows warping the garden pathways,
as the dark steps I climb are lit up
by his Eye magnetic to the moon,
his Eye magnetic to the moon.

I have not seen him when windows are mute
to whisper his name; on that moment
erroneous bats slip out through the sky.
His lair conceives my heart,
all hearts make the triangle he uses for a nose,
sniffing bloodways to my brain:
the bloodways are lit up by his Eye.

On a sudden appearance he tortures leaves?
flays branches and divides segments
the sun has drawn. I do not falter
– in the dark he fortifies.
His color is *green* green,
to distend him over the earth.
He does not fly.
You meet him while walking.

He is not easily enticed to manifestation,
but stony silence, petrified moments
– a transfiguration – will bring him out,
focused on the screen where all transfigured bodies are.
You must be humble to his fangs
that paw the moonball dissolving in the space

from the corner of your eye:
he will trick you otherwise
–into daylight, where you meet his double while running.
By night, the deltas of the moon-spilled planet
are stoned under his wriggling light.

By day, he chokes the sun.

THE LAST GANGSTER

Gregory Corso

Waiting by the window
my feet enwrapped with the dead bootleggers of Chicago
I am the last gangster, safe, at last,
waiting by a bullet-proof window.

I look down the street and know
the two torpedoes from St Louis.
I've watched them grow old
. . . guns rusting in their arthritic hands.

Poem from

DAILY LIFE

Julian Beck

this is my daily life
the subway is like the nozzle of a gun
all the boyscouts are dreaming of money and generals
and the girls with their turkish powder
that is all about murder and lonely death and dying
the golden girls are coming to dust
and i am dying

i do not berate the daily news
shape this dream into life
life as a dream
at lago di como in indochina
where they are shot by bushels
life is a dream
my whole life is a dream

it is a scandal to die as we do
full of tomato juice and chicken
marion elopes with a lover in bluejeans
whose tight pants reveal an abundant cock but we
                              know what'll happen
the flags of imperialism are made of barbed wire
joan is wrapped in the banner of bricks
the old crone cries that even the leaves of the elms
                              are like sores
the breast bursting with cancer
the hospitals jammed with untold debris

virgil pretending aeneas is a hero
that blood-letting big boy
who was never in love
who was never in love

D. SCARLATTI

Gregory Corso

Scarlatti counts his breath with a nasty
                    suicide wound;
He hip-hops in the sewer, a fiend
                 to unlistened powers.
He wears a dress coat, a top hat; has a cane
                  and goes hip-hop
thru demented halls.
  ears open for an old echo.

POUND AT SPOLETO

Lawrence Ferlinghetti

(Summer, 1965)

At noon I walked into a loge in the Teatro Melisso, the lovely Renaissance salle where the poetry readings and the chamber concerts were held every day of the Spoleto Festival, and suddenly saw Ezra Pound for the first time, sitting still as a Mandarin statue in a box at the back of the theatre, one tier up from the stalls. It was a shock. I didn't recognize him in the first instant, seeing only a striking old man in a curious pose, thin and long-haired, aquiline at 80, head tilted strangely to one side, lost in permanent abstraction. Thus he sat throughout the noon concert, never shifting his pose, eyes nowhere.

At 5 p.m. I went back to the box where I could see Pound again across from me. After three younger poets on-stage, he was scheduled to read from his box, and there he sat with an old friend (who held his papers) waiting, in the same pose as at noon, as if he had been there all afternoon. His head now bent, he regarded the knuckles of his hands, moving them a very little, expressionless. Otherwise he remained fixed. Only once, when everyone else in the full theatre was applauding someone on stage, did he rouse himself to clap, without looking up, mechanic-ally, as if stimulated by sound in a void. Pavlov. After almost an hour, his turn came. Or after a life.

Everyone in the hall rose, turned and looked back and up at Pound in his booth, applauding. The applause was prolonged and Pound tried to rise from his armchair. A microphone was partly in the way. He grasped the arms of the chair with his boney hands and tried to rise. He could not and he tried again and could not. His old friend did not try to help him. Finally she put a poem

76

in his hand and after at least a minute his voice came out. First the jaw moved and then the voice came out, inaudible. A young Italian pulled the stand-up mike up close to his face and held it there and the voice came over, frail but stubborn, higher than I had expected, a thin, soft monotone. The hall had gone silent at a stroke. The voice knocked me down, so soft, so thin, so frail, so stubborn still. I put my head on my arms on the velvet sill of the box. I was surprised to see a single tear drop on my knee. The thin, indomitable voice went on. Come to this! I went blind from the box, through the back door of it into the empty upper corridor of the theatre where they still sat turned to him, went down and out into the sunlight, weeping. . . . Up above the town, by the ancient aqueduct, the chestnut trees were still in bloom. Mute birds flew in the valley below, far off, the sun shone on the chestnut trees, and the leaves turned in the sun, and turned and turned and turned, and would continue turning. His voice went on, and on, through the leaves. . . .

"A NEW YEAR'S LETTER" A.L.

Andrei Voznesensky

These guests! heavy
   like hot-water bottles –
all in a row
   on their napkins
their hands lie, red
   like lobsters
on a plate. . . .
   And you! lost
among these enormous
   bowls, cooling
your cheek
   on a wine-glass –
off comes
   your shawl,
you're burning! 'It's so
   hot in here – '
But back at my place
   the window's
wide open, on the tall
   city, as onto
a garden – and the snow
   smelling like
apples, yellow
   Antonowka apples
its flakes
   suspended
in air,
   they don't move

they don't fall
   they're waiting,
weightless, static,
   observant
like small icon
   lamps, or tobacco
plants in summer:
   but they'll swing
in small arcs
   when touched
by a little foot
   in a smart Polish boot . . .
and the snow
and the smell of apples.

                                        −1961

                        English Version by
                        Anselm Hollo

PUMA IN CHAPULTEPEC ZOO

Gregory Corso

Long smooth slow swift soft cat
What score, whose choreography did you dance to
    when they pulled the final curtain down?
Can such ponderous grace remain
    here, all alone, on this 9X10 stage?
Will they give you another chance
    perhaps to dance the Sierras?
How sad you seem; looking at you
    I think of Ulanova
    locked in some small furnished room
    in New York, on East 17th Street
    in the Puerto Rican section.

HYMN TO THE GODDESS
SAN FRANCISCO
IN PARADISE

FROM Mountains & Rivers

Gary Snyder

If you want to live high get high

– Nihil C.

I

up under the bell skirt
caving over the soil
white legs flashing
   – amazed to see under their clothes they are
               naked
      this makes them sacred
& more than they are in their own shape
                free.

the wildest cock-blowing
   gang-fucking foul-tongued
      head chick
   thus the most so –

II

high town
high in the dark town

81

dream sex church
YAHWEH peyote spook
Mary the fish-eyed
            spotless,
            lascivious,
vomiting molten gold.

san fran sisco
hung over & swing down
                dancers on water
        oil slick glide
        shaman longshoremen
        magical strikes –
howls of the guardians rise from the waterfront.
– state line beauties those switcher engines
        leading waggons
warehouz of jewels and fresh fur

car leans
        on its downhill springs
                parked on mountainsides.
white minarets in the night
   demon fog chaos.
bison stroll on the grass.
        languid and elegant, fucking while standing
                young couples in silk
                        make-up on.

crystal towers   gleam for a hundred miles
            poison oak hedges, walld child garden
& the ring mountains holding a cool
        basin of pure evening fog
        strained thru the bridge
        gold and orange,
beams of cars wiser than drivers
   stream across promenades, causeways
        incensed exhaust.

smiling the City Hall Altar to Heaven
        they serve up the cock tail,
there is higher than nature in city

it spins in the sky.

III

quenching the blue flame
tasting the tea brought from China
cracking the fresh duck egg on white plate

passd out the gates of our chambers
over the clear miles, ships.
forever such ecstasy
              wealth & such beauty
              we live in the sign of Good Will . . .
(the white-robed saint trim my locks for
        a paltry sum . . . life is
        like free)
rolling lawns clippt and the smell of gum tree.
boiled crab from a saltwater vat.
                        rhine wine.
bison and elk of Chrysopylae
eels in those rocks in the wave
olive oil, garlic, soy, hard cheese.

Devas of small merit in Jambudvipa
Plucking sour berries to eat:
shall ascend to an eminence,
scanning the scene
      fog in
   from the Farallones
long ship low far below
   sliding under the bridge.
   bright white. red-lead.
        – blue of the sea.
   on that ship is me.

IV

– smilers all on the nod nap on cots
but the slither   & breakfree

83

                tossd slipper up on the toe
                  & the white thighs open
                  the flesh of the wet flower
                        LAW
crossed eyes gleam *come*
                flowery prints and
                yellow kettles in a row
                breast weight swelld down

kind chairmen smile around,
generals and presidents swallow
                        hoping   they too   can come . . .
            THERE IS NO WAY

            turn back dead tourist
            drop your crumb your funny passport
         – fall back richer spenders
            think you make with wild teenager
                    on hard forever
                    crust in jewel
                        – *you are too old.*
the san francisco fake front strip tease
phoney, sweaty,
last a minute and they stink and die

THIS LAND IS FOR THE HIGH
                & love is for ten thousand years.
                    (damnd square climbers give me pains)
them wilty blossoms on her sweaty brow . . .
            the flute and lute and drums

            policecars sireen down on Fillmore
            fog clears back away
            the police close in
                & shoot the loose
            & clouds are slipping by

& *hide it in your pockets.*

It all becomes plain sky.

HITCH HIKER

Jack Kerouac

'Tryna get to sunny Californy' –
    Boom. It's the awful raincoat
making me look like a selfdefeated self-
murdering imaginary gangster, an idiot in
a rueful coat, how can they understand
my damp packs – my mud packs –
        'Look Joh, a hitchhiker'
        'He looks like he's got a gun underneath
that I.R.A. coat'
        'Look Fred, that man by the road'
        'Some sexfiend got in print in 1938
in Sex Magazine' –
        'You found his blue corpse in a
greenshade edition, with axe blots'

1967

Fragment from

BOY WITH FACE
OF SOUR APPLES

Jeff Nuttall

Caught the last 84 from St Albans. Starkly empty. Yellow light
like spilled egg on five or six adolescent girls, very giggly, eating
fish and chips. More brightly dressed, less withit than London
girls. Odd how near London you can be and yet people get
distinctly rural. Get the impression they don't even see telly.
They do though. Oh yes they do.

Their males are seated typically apart, smoking. One, very
young, sits alone, has been pretty drunk. Is sober now although
groggy. Face where not in black shadow, is a sort of fruity green.
Front of his suit vile. Cheap M. & S. suit, no lapels, all laced and
crusted. Surely vomit on jacket, lower down maybe urine or
sperm . . . yechtt! Anyway a lacy lyric tracery of nausea. Thought
how sudden violent sights, however different, reduce me to my
constant identical neurosis, a fear that our oncoming suicide is
a fitting end to any creature whose vitality has so abated. This
boy seems to embody my idea of the species; sick, heartbroken,
swimming in his own filth, yet drawing from that filth and
humiliation the very vitality that is to carry out the manifest
promise of his youth . . . for he is youthful and beautiful. He is
like a wild flower in the light of a neon street lamp.

My mate Fred is another curiously typical case. Used to write.
Used to take an interest in jazz. Still plays occasionally. Married
to May who is largely what her name implies, a sensuous, slightly
tarty girl he met in the provinces, (where he lived for a time,)
who is now knocking it off with young Jim. He even tells me they
put Jim up overnight now and then and, lo and behold, at crack

86

of dawn May whips down to where Jim's curled up on the living room carpet (they don't own a spare bed) and copulates violently while poor old Fred remains upstairs pulling his wire in a strange mixture of self-pity, disappointment and vicarious pleasure. The sheer low pitch of his humiliation seems to be inextricable in his mind from the falsehoods and cowardices of the cold war. He seems to be acting out the low point of evolution by his own self-laceration. For this affair, oddly, carries his approval. He once told me he wanted to see just how much he could take and survive. I doubt if he will survive. He doesn't talk much now, seems infinitely less confident. I'm told it's often black despair. And yet dynamism is still there. Was there on the bus. The young, lost people had a definite explosive quality. I could find a turd wonderful. The sick boy should couple with Vanessa.

. . . self-pity was waiting for the 104 and seems to be inextricable in vomit . . . his violent mind plus a sudden self laceration . . . this affair vitaminised his approval . . . he sang the sun . . . Radiocars once told me he wanted a kind smile . . . see how much he could know Jebb . . . your doubt will survive . . . soft as a kitten . . . talk so much smoke, man . . . infinitely less confident man was . . . oh . . . a drip . . . often black despair to see Simon Jebb . . . dynamism is still a necklace of glittering beads . . . was there on the sunspun angelbitch . . . lost people gone a little . . . no more definite explosive SLIMLINES . . . Aldermaston Easter quality . . . I could find a morning pink . . . huge worn turd . . . wonderful . . . the sick navy should couple with last night's glitter. . . .

She was waiting for the 104 on Barnet Hill and the morning vomited Yes all over her shoulder . . . smile, the look is glamorous but not formal. Wear the complete outfit . . . tabard top plus a sudden kindness . . . VITAMINISED IRON JELLOIDS PUT NEW LIFE INTO YOU 4/6 and 7/6 a bottle sang the sun, came crashing radiocars up Barnet Hill, bowled blinding to a stop at traffic lights . . . and a kind smile.

' . . . not seen you . . . some time. Oh pretty well. Yes . . . to see Jebb. You know Jebb. Well he knows you . . . ' and thank you for your hair soft as a kitten yet it HOLDS HOLDS HOLDS . . . 'upstairs . . . want to smoke . . . man who followed you at the college was . . . oh . . . a drip . . . complete drip . . . to see Simon Jebb. Yes that's right. I knew you knew him . . . ' skirt, add a neckful of glittering beads or a pair of pretty earrings. Make up for soft . . . soft soft you sunspun angelbitch, gone a little banthebeatnikbomb since last time. No more pencil SLIMLINES. No more careful lipstick. Swapped for Aldermaston Easter-morning Pink (your banjo will hardly know you). Huge worn duffle, navy, and her hair and inner labyrinth repeats in morning bustop last night's glitter-bustop-castle (apple-boy-cum-Schristmastree of cold cooked bauballs) spins and hives a tower of Babeling Jerusalem, its honeycomb of antworn, kingcarved, catacombs all echoing with the winds and songs and corridor whispers and secrets (. . . hear the dead pass lovenotes, kiss a rendezvous in stripped top corridor Versailles and sound and reek of stale perfume and hear at Knossos . . . yes . . . a quite distinct far titter of tombed painted courtesans, bullmaidens, sifting sound like dust . . . . Her mound / wrapped twist / wild Babel-tower of tunnelled hair sung songs of Yes and found a punctuating shriek here . . . and here . . . and here is where I get off . . . no, it doesn't matter. See ya . . . 'But are you awfully unhappy?'

'My husband is a keen athlete . . . running, football, tennis and swimming. When we married he insisted that we must severely restrict his sexual activities.'

ANS: 'Tell him to sleep with his goal posts in future.'

The 104 went up the Highgate Road carrying in it
(a)   A hat of hair.
(b)   A nightful laced with unshot sperm.
(c)   That huge sadsilent unplayed chord that jangles out those ole disintegration bloo-hoo-hoos.

Passengers unfamiliar with the above method of communication are informed that all buses between the hours of 12 midnight on Sunday, February 9, 1964 and 12 midnight on Tuesday, February 12, 1964 contained a number of miracles.
. . . smile the glamorous morning . . . tabard top plus a sudden Vanessa . . . I don't think kindness, vitaminised iron into any human being . . .the sun came crashing singularly beautiful, really blinding kind smile . . . Yes . . . to see is a knock out . . . thank you for getting on the same bus . . . upstairs . . . went to . . . together . . . her hair was . . . oh . . . a drip . . . glittering beads or wild, messy soft sunspun beatnikbomb . . . no more golden tunnel . . . no more tower of morning Pink . . .banjo duffle Babel or the Goonshow . . . last night's glitter made a replica of cooked balls . . . babeling Albert Memorial 'uman honeycomb . . .

kingcarved catacombs echoing with the morning sun . . . hear the dead beating down on the whole rendezvous . . . top-corridor hillside bursting through a reek of stale perfume . . . front window of dust . . . wild Babel bus making marvellous effects . . . sung songs and found a shriek in her hair-do . . . she reminded me of matter . . . unhappy young people . . . my husband is too early . . . sexual activities seem to have almost completely evaporated . . . tell him to sleep brightly in 1956 . . . the 104 went up the Highgate Road carrying all bomb . . . a hat of hair not needed . . . unplayed chord jangles out help even then . . . disintegration died with Trad jazz . . . passengers, still a few left . . . a bus moving a dirty person   Vanessa at the bus-stop this morning . . . a very good morning to see Vanessa. I don't think I know any human being so singularly beautiful. She really is a knock-out. We are getting on the same bus and we rode down Barnet Hill together. Her hair, which was chic the last time I saw it, was wild, messy and all piled on top in a great golden, tunnelled heap that reminded me of a sort of Tower of Babel or the Goonshow character who made a replica of the Albert Memorial in 'uman 'air. The morning sun was beating down on the whole hillside, bursting through the front windows of the bus making marvellous effects in her marvellous hair-do. She reminded me of that generation of young people I was too early to belong to and who now seem to have almost completely evaporated. They flared brightly in 1956 when Suez had made us all bomb happy (not that I needed any help even then) and died with the Trad jazz craze. They were great kids. There are still a few left and Vanessa is one of them. I find it tremendously moving that such a dirty person should be so graceful. She is also kind, with the extreme charm of attitude that I find implicit in Gainsborough's brush. She was on her way to see Simon Jebb.

Now Simon Jebb . . . there's a right nut case. When he first approached me in a jazz club with an elaborate bow I could scarcely believe my eyes. Ginger hair in a pudding basin dome. Shy, half-closed eyes with long blonde lashes. Huge, buck teeth, weird, brightly coloured clothes and this unnerving caricature manner. Whilst being about fifteen years of age he was pretty drunk. He is still pretty drunk, whilst aged about twenty-one.

Later there was a gang of them. The odd, bewildered, edgy children of left-wing intellectuals whose 'sensible living' had cast their children headlong into the most violent idiocies. They all lived in a car. I think they were part of the car. Jebb, Loopy, Fiona, the cadaverous Fiona, and that other strange beautiful boy whose clothes were so brightly affected they almost amounted to drag. He runs a pop group now.

Vanessa obviously loves Jebb wildly and too maternally. She talked ceaselessly about him and his problems but she was nice to me. She smiled . . . and brother, I can use it these days.

I live on buses much of the time. They are curious microcosms, mobile, violent, deadly dull and colourful.

UNTITLED POEM

Jack Kerouac

Hey listen you poetry audiences
If you dont shut up
And listen to the potry,
See . . . we'll set a guy at the gate
To bar all potry haters
Forevermore

Then, if you dont like the subject
Of the poem that the poit
Is readin, geen, why dont
You try Marlon Brando
Who'll open your eyes
With his cry

James Dean is dead? –
   Aint we all?
   Who aint dead –

John Barrymore is dead

Naw San Francisco is dead
– San Francisco is bleat
   With the fog

1956?

CAPRICORN IS A WOUNDED KNEE

Philip Lamantia

No wonder the night is smeared with ectoplasm
eagle's blood flows over the planets
and we cast a spell for seven hawks to fly out of the moon
that silence may prevail
to so startle the noisy villagers
for us to hear the songs that break
from the lips of the air

SEA CHANTY

Gregory Corso

My mother hates the sea,
my sea especially,
I warned her not to;
it was all I could do.
Two years later
the sea ate her.

Upon the shore I found a strange
yet beautiful food;
I asked the sea if I could eat it,
and the sea said I could.
– Oh, sea, what fish is this
so tender and so sweet? –
– Thy mother's feet – was its answer.

UNTITLED POEM

Pablo Picasso

the fringes of candlelight
making their calculations on
the taut fabric
of stone woods   huddled
among the groves of fig
trees casting their
reckonings under
the belly-button of the mortar hoarse
with cries and mending
slid under the door
writ out with fat brush above
the fragment of syrupy sky
posted as
sentinel   edge of the crib
sparkling out

crumbs and wolf-whistles
over the house
pitched into the sea the house
fly in the land
scape   fried in the pan
freezing his hands
on the water-faucet
                spigot.

MAY DAY SPEECH—1970

Jean Genet

I must begin with an explanation of my presence in the United States.

In my situation with regard to the administration, there is an element of unreality I must take into account. As it happens, for the last two months I have moved from place to place without being disturbed, my entry into the country was made under unconventional circumstances, my way of life, here and elsewhere, is that of a vagabond and not of a revolutionary, my behavior itself is out of the ordinary, so that I must be very careful when I speak in the name of the Black Panther Party which is after all attached to this country, whose habits are not nomadic and which protects itself by means declared to be legal, and with real weapons. I mean that no unreality should creep into my own statements, for it would be prejudicial to the Black Panther Party and to Bobby Seale who is really in a real jail made of stones and concrete and steel.

My own freedom of speech and movement must not be a game, a matter of whim: which is one of the reasons I assent to the necessities of the Panthers.

The second point I should like to make is linked to the first: racism in the United States is spreading fast. I had noticed it upon arrival. It was the first thing I saw, but gradually, living here, I had supposed as well that I made out other and healthier behavior, in which racism played no part. And then occurred the events in the New Haven courtroom. From the moment I came into the courtroom, I glimpsed American racism – in other words, anti-black racism, in all its violence. Coming into the courtroom with my black friends of the Black Panther Party, a policeman, without consulting me, led me to the first row of seats, in that part of the court where there were only whites. Thanks to the insistence of my black friends, I was able to sit with them. This may seem to you an insignificant episode, but for me, being there and being its pseudo-beneficiary, it was a sign I immediately translated. And whereas Hilliard and Emory were arrested for contempt of court by reading a paper, I myself, who had read another paper before the court, was simply removed from the courtroom, but left free.

Another event occurred, a few days later, confirming this observation: a black friend of mine whom I cannot name, some whites and I were getting into a TWA plane. A policeman, in the passageway leading to the plane, ordered the black to open his suitcase. His suitcase contained only three shirts and three pairs of pants, and he was allowed into the plane; but the policeman changed his mind, and, with an escort of five more cops, after having shown his card, forced our friend to get off the plane. None of the three whites, myself included, was treated this rudely. (Fortunately there are other airlines besides TWA.)

My interpretation is therefore as follows: I have not been touched because I am white and because I offer no threat of danger to American Society. The blacks of course are black, therefore guilty of being black, and the Black Panther Party is a threat to the middle-class order of America.

I now come to what seems to me very important: the quality of the relations of leftist organizations with the Black Panther Party. Here it seems to me that the whites must provide a new dimension to politics – delicacy of heart. You must realize that there is no question of sentimentality here, but of a delicacy in our relations with men who do not have the same rights as ourselves. Even if their rights are acknowledged by the laws of the country, the blacks are far from full possession of those rights, as I have suggested in speaking of New Haven, and the Black Panther Party still less so. There exists, as you know, as you see around you every day, a *de facto* discrimination. We can observe this everywhere, even and especially in the unions, even among the workers, even in the universities. It is therefore quite obvious that the white radicals must adopt a line of behavior which will tend to eliminate their own privileges. As for the other whites, it is understood that if they cling so closely to their whiteness, it is in death itself that they will find it. The whitest white man, for the moment, is a dead white man.

If the pride of the blacks and of the Black Panther Party, and sometimes their arrogance (but what is to be said of the arrogance of the whites, and of their brutality with regard not only to the blacks but to the whole world!), if that pride, I say, is the result of a new political awareness, this awareness is still too new for them not to be quickly provoked when they and their positions are contested. They have a tendency – and they are right to be suspicious – to see in that contestation a desire of the white man, more or less conscious, to dominate them once again. It all works out as if, to the correctness of their ideas when they are correct, the whites were adding one more element of authoritarianism in the expression of these ideas, so that the blacks can see a nascent imperialism in this phenomenon as well. This habit of domination is communicated in the white man's ideas and perhaps is what he calls his American dynamism.

It is essential, then, for the white radicals to act frankly, no doubt, but delicately, in their relations with the blacks, for, once again, a black man risks jail for a trivial gesture, whereas between a white man who makes the same gesture and the authorities, something like a complicity is established. A complicity of which the white man is also unconscious, but which the black cannot help feeling. To refuse to accept this as a fact of the matter is to reveal one's arrogance, brutality, lazy-mindedness or simple stupidity.

It is quite true that blacks and whites have a gulf of 400 years of contempt to bridge. There was a so-called superiority on the side of the whites, but the whites did not suspect that they were being observed, in silence it is true, but all the more closely observed. Today, the blacks have drawn from this silent observation a profound knowledge of the white man, and the converse is not the case.

It is therefore up to the whites to undertake an understanding of the blacks, and, I repeat, this can be done only in a delicacy of relations, when blacks and whites decide upon a political action in common – as revolutionaries.

Up till now, the blacks found among white men only two means of expression: brutal domination, or a distant, rather contemptuous paternalism. Another way must be found. The one I have suggested is another way.

The blacks ask for nothing but equality in relations. That is clear. Given the disproportion of the white man's privileges, the whites, if they are determined to have a relation of equality, are obliged to behave as I have said. Not abject, but attentive, alert to what continues to wound the black man still, after these terrible 400 years.

Perhaps we must do away with symbols and with symbolic gestures. I am not speaking of the emblems whose real content is of no great consequence, but of symbols themselves, as a substitution for a revolutionary action. (Provisional definition of a *revolutionary action:* any action capable of suddenly breaking down the bourgeois order with a view to achieving a socialist order.)

The American left, and particularly that fraction of the left which calls itself radical, has the possibility of no longer making empty gestures but of realizing actions. In a sense it has a field of action, and that is its combat for the liberation of Bobby Seale and its aid to the Black Panther Party.

The symbols refer to an action which has taken place, not to an action which is to come, since any action which is realized (I am speaking of revolutionary actions) cannot seriously nourish itself on familiar examples. Hence every revolutionary action has that freshness of a new beginning, a new world.

But a gesture, or a group of symbolic gestures are idealistic in this sense, that they saturate the men who perform them or who adopt the symbol, preventing them from performing real actions of irreversible power. I should say that a symbolic attitude is both the liberal's good conscience and a situation which suggests that everything has been tried for the revolution. It is better to perform real actions, of apparently small scope, than theatrical and futile manifestations. One must never forget this when one knows that the Black Panther Party seeks to be armed, and armed with real weapons.

To speak to its members about pacifism or non-violence would be a criminal act. For it would be to preach to them an evangelical virtue which no white man is capable of applying or of attaching to his own experience.

I have said that the American left, if it wants to be revolutionary, has the possibility of performing real actions, with regard to Bobby Seale, in collaboration with the Black Panther Party. To refuse this, would be to accept here in the United States the outbreak of a kind of Dreyfus Affair. Perhaps still more damaging than the Dreyfus Affair in France and in Europe. It is time to decide whether the intellectuals are keeping quiet because Bobby Seale is guilty or because he is black and chairman of the Black Panther Party, and if the intellectuals are afraid of the threats made by Agnew against those who help or encourage the Party. And everything, here, seems to indicate that we are turning away from Bobby Seale because he is black, and in the same way that Dreyfus was guilty because he was a Jew.

There was a time in France when the guilty man was The Jew. Here, there was such a time, and there is still, when the guilty man is The Negro.

Naturally, this parallel with the Dreyfus Affair cannot be pursued point by point. And I must admit that up till now, in America, there has been no Clemenceau, no Jaures, and especially, among the intellectuals, no Zola to write 'J'Accuse'. A 'J'Accuse' which would bear witness against the courts of your country and against the majority of whites, who have remained racists.

When we speak of the Black Panther Party, we must also realize that in a year and a half, police repression has risen from 1 to 7. I mean that the number of police actions must be multiplied by seven.

Another thing concerns me: fascism. We often hear the Black Panthers speak of fascism, and it is hard for the whites to accept the word. This is because it requires a great effort of imagination on the part of white men to realize that the blacks live under an oppressive and fascist regime. For them, this fascism is not the consequence of the American government alone, but also of the entire white community, which is truly privileged.

Here, the whites are not directly oppressed, but the blacks are, in mind and sometimes in body.

In this oppression, the blacks are right to accuse the whites as a whole, and they are right to speak of fascism.

We whites are living perhaps in a liberal democracy, but the black man lives, like it or not, under a paternalist, authoritarian, imperialistic regime. It is important to spread the love of freedom among you. But the whites are afraid of freedom. It is too strong a drink for them. They suffer yet another fear, which keeps growing – which is to discover the intelligence of the black man.

Yet I have hope for the black people and for the revolution undertaken by the Black Panther Party. First of all, all the peoples of the Third World are increasingly conscious of the revolutionary necessity; secondly, the whites, and even the Americans, and even

Johnson and what has come after, can transform themselves.

Personally, I place a certain trust in man's nature, even in the nature of the most limited man. The enterprise of the Black Panther Party continues to grow, the public is increasingly numerous which understands them, and the white intellectuals will perhaps support them: that is why I am among you today.

As for Bobby Seale, I repeat, there must not be another Dreyfus Affair. Therefore I count on you, on all of you, to spread the contestation abroad, to speak of Bobby Seale in your families, in the universities, in your courses and classrooms: you must contest and occasionally contradict your professors and the police themselves.

And, I say it once more for it is important, what is at stake are no longer symbolic gestures, but real actions.

And if it comes to this, I mean if the Black Panther Party asks it of you, you must desert your universities, leave your classrooms in order to carry the word across America in favor of Bobby Seal and against racism.

The life of Bobby Seale, the existence of the Black Panther Party, come first – ahead of your diplomas. You must now – and you have the physical, material, and intellectual means to do so – you must now face life directly and no longer in comfortable aquariums – I mean the American universities – which raise goldfish capable of no more than blowing bubbles.

The life of Bobby Seale depends on you. Your real life depends on the Black Panther Party.

*

('Appendix' – not read in New Haven, but written for that purpose.)

What they call American civilization will disappear. It is actually already dead, for it is based on contempt. For instance, contempt of the rich for the poor, of white for black, etc. All civilizations based on contempt must necessarily disappear. And I'm not speaking of contempt in terms of morals but in terms of function: what I mean to say is that contempt as an institution contains its own dissolution, and the dissolution of what it engenders.

You will say that I am mixing into America's affairs: the thing

100

is that I am following America's own example of mixing into everybody else's business all over the world. After meddling with Korea she meddled in Vietnam, then Laos, and now Cambodia, and I do so with America.

I would like to denounce somewhat haphazardly the following institutions, and above all the Press. The news as it is presented to Americans is criminal because it is presented through rose-colored glasses or not presented at all. The New York Times is lying, Look Magazine is lying by omission, by carefulness or cowardice. Naked truth scares them. New Yorker Magazine is lying too, because of mental deficiency. Television is lying too when it abstains from giving the true motivations which led three black people to ambush four white cops. Since the Press has all the means of information and yet refuses to fully inform, it is responsible for the Americans' thundering stupidity.

Now the Church. Born of an Oriental fable whose original meaning was diverted by the Occidentals, it has become another tool of repression, especially here against the blacks to whom it preaches an evangelical softness in order to respect the master – the white – and by the Old Testament it also promises the fires of hell to those who rebel.

The 'charitable' institutions, controlled by all-powerful companies – the Ford Foundation or Rockefeller Institute, etc. – who control those they allegedly help.

The unions, of which I barely have to speak, since they are your enemies, and, more pathetic, the workers, who are their own enemies. In order to compensate for being at the end of the line, the victims of their bosses, they take refuge in an idiotic comfort and in aggressive racism against the blacks.

I'm not forgetting the university. Or the universities. They teach you a false culture, in which the only recognized values are quantitative. They are not content to reduce you to being one digit in a number, for instance when creating 500,000 engineers, but the University cultivates in you the need for security, tranquility and quite naturally educates you to serve the bosses, and, beyond them, the politicians, whose intellectual mediocrity you are well aware of. So much so that you, who want to be scientists, will end up in an armchair, at the table – but at the end of the table – of a mediocre politician. And you will be proud of it.

I continue: another institution – the promoters of commercials

101

and newspaper ads. Newspapers are filled with idiotic ads. So are the television channels. And the promoters, by threatening to boycott both newspapers and television, make the directors tremble with fear. So that what actually moves you, in the United States, is a gigantic tremor. Everyone is afraid of everyone else. The strongest is afraid of the weakest, the least asinine is afraid of the most asinine. What is still called American dynamism is nothing but a big shiver shaking the whole country.

I shall finish up this list with one major institution: the Police. They too make people tremble. They threaten, but they too are trembling. They are not very sure of themselves. Three days ago old Johnson was saying that the Warren Commission was wrong in designating Oswald as the only guilty party in the Kennedy murder. Now the most ironic thing is that it was this supreme master of the Police, this very same Johnson, who cautioned the Warren Commission originally. This contradiction, or this reversal, might provoke one gigantic burst of laughter – at any rate, in Peking they must be laughing very loud – but over here, in the end, it's very sad.

19

Lawrence Ferlinghetti

with bells for hooves in sounding streets
that terrible horse the unicorn

came on
and cropped a medlar from a tree
and where he dropped the seed
sprang up a virgin

oh she sprang up upon his back
and rode off tittering to a stair
where pieces of string lay scattered
everywhere
Now when she saw the string so white
so lovely and so beautiful
and looking like
Innocence itself
she got down and reached for a nice
straight piece

but it had a head
and it bit
her beautiful place
So (she said)

this is how it all began
Next time I'll know
But it was too late and they buried her

HOW TO MEDITATE

Jack Kerouac

               – lights out –
fall, hands a-clasped, into instantaneous
ecstasy like a shot of heroin or morphine,
the gland inside of my brain discharging
the good glad fluid (Holy Fluid) as
I hap-down and hold all my body parts
down to a deadstop trance – Healing
all my sicknesses – erasing all – not
even the shred of a 'I-hope-you' or a
Loony Balloon left in it, but the mind
blank, serene, thoughtless. When a thought
comes a-springing from afar with its held-
forth figure of image, you spoof it out,
you spuff it off, you fake it, and
it fades, and thought never comes – and
with joy you realize for the first time
'Thinking's just like not thinking –
So I don't have to think
   any
   more'

1967

THERE'S AN
OLD STORY

Antonin Artaud

There's an old story about charred monkeys keeps coming back
to me when I think about the stories of this collapsing world
    I am
still a tenant of, though not for
long I hope
where the few real friends I have, friends not so much of
my work as of my life, give the effect of a last small
island of consciousness
aboard the ark, even if we suppose that this means nowadays
some mere raft of flesh & bones,
so:
aboard the ark on the eve of the big splash, on the verge of
strangulation,
asphyxia of putrid meat rushing up over the
brain mind
& smothering it.

A frightful wrath leaps up on every side, where,
I do believe, the big social problems are nothing much
next to a certain physiological irritation in the epidermis
skin & bones, something very few have seen
that will drown out all else soon,
for this is no mere rage of the mind,
not even a rage of the heart, no,
this time we have a body rage
the rage of this great stepchild of the history of
man as well as beast:
                the b o d y.

Many big splashes went down the drain of history,
many inexpiable disasters that stopped short and
however inexpiable they may have felt
agreed to throw in the sponge
because the body was always
being kept out of the rumble
& it was mind, not body, that ran those revolutions

AS IF revolution were a thing that got
underway then stuck to the rules
like a ballet or the pawns on a
checkerboard
& you finally tucked it away in your coat pocket
like the pawns on a
checkerboard.
So, as long as history has been history, mind not body has led
the ballet – no corps even in the corps du ballet.

The mind with its monopoly on values & things
which upsets all value of things
AS IF there were ideas & things, with even
the body being submitted to a ploughshare, plus
ideas & principles – and
a body that is supposed to be Idea.

So that I Artaud suspect I am a horse & not a man
I am not that suspect on all fours being kicked in irons
now & then, but I am a certain being so iron in force
no horse could suspect I was a man
nor any man force me up, once on all fours.

So certain I was I was a horse
I made & nailed on
4 iron shoes
being no man but a certain horse kicked
by all who suspect I am a man & so force me
not to be a horse that I am forced
up in the air with all 4 edges flying & I can

kick like hell
& snort out both nostrils

& they can't trip me up on words because I
Won't be saying anything.

And what am I trying to say now:
What the fuck am I here for?

– Translated by David Rattray

A PASTORAL FETISH

Gregory Corso

Old MacDonald wears clod-hoppers
in his walk through field of lilac and dandelion
A storm-trooper, like a Klee twittering machine, he stomps:
Crunch one lilac here; crunch another dandelion there,
here, there, everywhere (he's got no mercy at all)
crunch crunch here and a crunch crunch there
crunch everywhere. . . .

There comes a time when he's got to stop
take off his shoes; go to bed . . .
ah, that's when Old MacDonald's in his glory.
Green blood and mud-caked leather he digs the most.
He makes it a habit to sleep his nose by his toes
so that all night long he could snore in the sticky smell
of murdered lilac and dandelion.
It's the old bastard's greatest kick.

MEAT SCIENCE ESSAYS: DEFENSE OF JAYNE MANSFIELD

Michael McClure

This essay was written before the death of Marilyn Monroe the Perfect Mammal – and I send her my farewell in another book. . . .

Jayne Mansfield is a member of a black American tradition that stretches from Poe to her – and includes Thoreau and many known and unremembered beings.

There's no more contrivance to Jayne Mansfield than there is to Thoreau or Poe. I'm not speaking of her art as actress. I speak of her as a being. Thoreau and Poe are similar creatures – they capture human imagination by their *existence*. That they catch thought doesn't mean they are synthetic or contrived. I think the three have a secret darkness in common.

I only think of her physical beauty. With Poe we speak of the beauty of his physical mind, and with Thoreau we think of the physiology of his desire for freedom.

A blackness and sexuality and mystery cloudily surrounds all lambs of this world – there is an intense secrecy beneath everything soft. This is not purely an American thing – tho we see much of it here – there is an alienation of creature from creature on our continent, and it fosters mysteries. The great French poet Antonin Artaud is one of the lambs of Europe.

There is nothing more synthetic in the body of Jayne Mansfield than there is in the writing or brain of Artaud. Artaud is a warchief of history as well as a lamb. Artaud is as real a warchief as Crazy Horse and Jayne Mansfield is as much a black lamb as Artaud. Artuad fought for eternal truth and beauty and the immortality of his super-masochistic soul. We only dimly know and faintly guess for what Crazy Horse died – his mind is a foreign universe forever closed. (What sight of American mountains and Bison did he envision over Custer's corpse?) I know that Artaud is a lamb and a warchief and I know Jayne Mansfield is at least a lamb. My eyes and body tell me she is a lamb. If she were contrived her capturing of my love would be more strange. In the dark tradition it is possible that the most sure members are not conscious of the mystery they carry in their physique or words.

The tradition of blackness is a heritage of health carried unconsciously by innocents. The darkness is *Love* that is driven undercover into their bodies or souls and spirits. It makes them darkly luminous. They are the carriers of a lost and necessary health that is desired by those they attract. The innocents, the lambs, that carry darkness must be understood and loved!

Poe, Thoreau, Mansfield are trappers of men's imaginations – whether they do it by bodies of words on the page or by lovely gestures.

How does the lover of every spring flower, awaiting the specific day of each blossoming, become driven to write on civil disobedience? How does a poet of such fine sensibility as Poe's become involved with the music of decay? His sensibility is lamblike. (Read *The Narrative Of A. Gordon Pym.*) Poe's love of clarity and science fastened on more than the decor of love-of-death; his secret writings are a view of the universe that he came to by inspired and idealistic thought. The true-black that lies unnoticed in so many beings is healthiness and a striving for health – it is the desire to see, be, speak, and disobey.

The importance of a work of art notwithstanding (Jayne Mansfield leaves no works of art), there is a great importance to each dark being.

Marlon Brando is singular, but he does not contain blackness. He enacted the desire to act and we trembled. Brando and Jayne Mansfield are both temporal – and Artaud, Poe, Thoreau are immortal. All of them cause us to tremble. There are always overlappings of mortality and immortality, and art and being and being and art . . . it cannot be unraveled because it need not be. There's a secret: *we are all creatures of talents and qualities* – some humans attract our imaginations because of a darkness that they glow outwards, and we long for it.

Jayne Mansfield draws by the black mystery of her physical presence. I know it is a soundness and a wholesomeness I see in her and I admire it. It is strange that men put down her health – it is so mysterious and dark because it is rare, and more so because it is suppressed by most who have it.

Surely most loving men would want Jayne Mansfield's love. In Latin America crowds shout for the sight of her breasts, and she shows herself.

Jayne Mansfield is ambitious – how black and simple and lovely her ambitions are. How straight she must be with herself sometimes! She looks so sane! There's something clean and simple about ambition – about having your body and winning with it.

The artist may be a catalyst but how can he work, what may he work with, without the sight of the talents and qualities of men and women? How few show themselves as simply as Jayne Mansfield. Perhaps all suppressions are related – and much beauty is a luminescence of the darkly unseen. But that is not a reason to hide – it is a reason to bring to light – there will always be a new beauty recoverable! Where are the bones of Crazy Horse?

Jayne Mansfield's secret and her darkness and her wholesomeness are her sexuality. Thoreau's mystery was his health too – his desire to expand and disobey and withdraw at the pleasure of his own dilation and longings. Thoreau and Mansfield are dark because both must hold within what they should be free to display – it is only dark because it is undercover. The abundance of darkness manifests itself upon the face of Mansfield and the pages of H. D. Thoreau. What mass of Thoreau's thoughts and feelings are left unsaid? . . . What he didn't say is nearly apparent.

Darkness is upon Jayne Mansfield's face and her arms and fingers. Even there she must hold back to pass censors and creators of suppression. Sexuality is plainly black and mysterious in itself. Sex in darkness and sex in light is always black. We live in an age that darkens sex and often brings hunger to the fields of plenty.

The Greeks, responding to the universe, were lovers of sleek and firm flesh – it was at hand for them – for eye, for touches, for kisses and garlands. They loved exaggeration of sexuality – they consecrated temples to the breasts and buttocks of Venus. They loved the supernaturality of huge breasts and they were intent on the loveliness of buttocks. They would believe that the torso and limbs and smile of Jayne Mansfield are supernatural.

If Jayne Mansfield's body is Spirit, and I think that it is true of all, then she is supernatural! Her breasts and beauty and body are to be admired. Jayne Mansfield and all lovely sexual beings are held back to a half-sexuality and they may not achieve completed voluptuousness. There is health in her that is half-manifested – but that is not her fault; *she tries*. She is blocked from completion and fulfillment.

Athens would worship her as Buenos Aires did – or more, Athens would make statues of her.

The secret and mystery of Jayne Mansfield is apparent to the puritanic – the blackness is obvious. She wears the black fur of her body and is crowned by whiteness.

The fame that she has is accounted to the shameless wet-mouthedness of her beauty – but I mean that too . . . it's part of her mystery and supernaturality . . . the blackness of her health catches at us in our dreams.

Give Jayne Mansfield roses and lilies, and rare honey and juice of apricots and liquors more secret than drambuie and the whitest most perfect bread. Let Anacreon praise her, and the scholars in two thousand years shall argue whether the verses are silver or golden. She is a dark creature – let the words that come from her lips be remembered; perhaps if she is *cherished* then words of unearthly wisdom will accompany her beauty. We must not imagine what she is or expect what she is. Leave her to BE and show us her supernaturality.

Free Jayne Mansfield and let her wholly manifest herself! What may she show us of love? – she who is by exaggeration of body and spirit so much a creature of love!

That which is beautiful is not synthetic tho it must sometimes come out on a field of falseness – she was borne into it by her body. Let the darkness out to the light. . . .

II. MANSFIELD & HARLOW
Oh, lamb, lamb, could I but remember
the poem I wrote for you

112

in the book that now lies burnt.

Jean Harlow I didn't destroy the poem I wrote for you. And you don't need a defense.

Jayne Mansfield you are THE BLACK. Jean Harlow you are *La Plus Blanche* – the most white. Marilyn Monroe is THE MAMMAL. Jayne Mansfield alone needs protection and a champion – but you are all creatures of love.

Jean Harlow, were you a better actress than Mansfield or Monroe? . . . I only saw you twice. Once in a film you stepped between Laurel and Hardy in a hotel lobby – you glided between the thick and thin of comedy like a woman of velvet between two shadows. I was stirred as they were – and they didn't put it on. I saw part of CHINA DOLL – I couldn't watch it, even for your sake, or *for* your sake I wouldn't watch it. But I hoarded pictures of you . . . they are locked tight in my brain. I have never found a biography of you (– nor of Lana Turner, tho I've read her love letters in the newspapers and they should be printed as a tribute to the warmth of women). I don't care if you could act or not. I fell in love with you in a half minute – your greatness of being brings about love. Some see you as tough whore or nymph – but they see you with the same eyes. You are a unity!

*

I wrote the poem with a still of her profile before me, but it was not her face that caused me to feel loveliness – the sight of her walking came to my eyes. When she stepped Jean Harlow did not touch the earth – but she did touch it – and she didn't pretend that her toes were not there on it. She passed by with liquid sexual grace of a woman. She didn't take the grace-pose an actress makes before the camera for a million million admirers in futurity. She moved and smiled with the whiteness of life, and she turned to stare! The still photo pictures only her face and a sensitive sleekness to eye, to chin and to gaze – and a yearning in her neck and shoulder.

A poem I wrote for Jayne Mansfield, and burned, was caused by a photo I saw of her. She lay naked with a towel over her buttocks. She looked up smiling her lovely smile of huge lips and white teeth. Her enormity and supernaturality stretched out upon the boardwalk like a mysterious fleshly first-aid kit of love.

113

. . . She had some good thing that was badly needed and she gave it freely. It seemed that what she had – her medicine – was more than aid; it must also be a challenge. To love Jayne Mansfield would be to find the supernormal in yourself – to reply to her love. And is not that supernormal a true norm? She seems like a red-cross lamb of love with darkness gleaming through delicacy, slim arms, and huge bosoms, into the sunlight. In another snapshot she holds a tiny teddy bear to her breasts – its nose presses through the opening of a transparent negligee to her nipples – while she looks down smiling with her platinum hair piled up on her head like a waif. And I've seen stranger pictures too. I like her eyes. I always wonder what she *might* do in life – if she were free to do it. What public demonstration or celebration of love would she make from her blackness if she were free to do it?

Jean Harlow is the whole moist woman and white beast – she seems only to bring simple love – she is sophisticated and the love is still simple – she wants to bring and receive pleasure with pointed highlights of emotion. Though one is black and one is white, neither Mansfield nor Harlow would injure or tear at a lover. Jean Harlow makes no challenge – she asks for a partner and protector, and though her body is spiritual she longs with a soul we all understand. The breasts and vast smile of Jayne Mansfield are a meat-spirit that we can barely conceive of.

The sight of Jean Harlow, womanly and striding, makes gentle concussions that become immortal statuaries in the memory. The appearance of Jayne Mansfield is a sexual occasion. She does not disguise the event, she makes it for us. She does all that can be done with an instant of speech or photograph – sexuality flows from her in undulant and almost comic fullness and implies what is still there. She seems to mock herself with good humor and surplus. It is wrong to think the dark tradition is without humor or full of gloom – Poe is one of the comic writers . . . even *Walden* has humorous passages. And why is Mark Twain immortal?

Would a small child seeing Jean Harlow in a film remember? Or would he think, in his simpler world, that all women are like Harlow – or that they should be. Jean Harlow has a gift of common and almost perfect love – there is nothing *unattainable* in her. She has a shadowiness – but it is the darkness of a comedy that depends on a higher vision of her soul – her sexuality is white and simple and not dark. Harlow has no *demand* or ecstasy of the flesh – but she searches for feeling and has a gift of intense and gentle pleasure. I think a child *might* remember Mansfield more . . . in the night.

Perhaps Harlow is most to the man or youth who has suffered from love.

And there is Marilyn Monroe who is a classical balance of men's desires; she is the most understandable for she contains all – she is no specialist but a perfection – she is understood at once but the understanding is not casual. Monroe is neither black nor white – she's rosy.

Harlow shows the simple greatness of women – she is an embodiment of simplicity and flow of pleasure. There are more beautiful *eyes* than Harlow's – but there is no more beautiful creature.

Mansfield brings to memory faces and bodies of childlike challenging sexual ecstacy. But should it be challenge? Harlow makes me think of tender pleasures without threat. There are huger breasts than Jayne Mansfield's – but there are few beings like her, and the others hide their Blackness behind a cold face.

Let us give honor to beauty in all beings and set men and women free so they may make their secret selves apparent. Let's not block Jayne Mansfield's unmade acts of sexual and voluptuous greatness, nor any other creature's. What would be the fulfillment of any person's qualities and talents? The Greeks were wise with their beauties and praised supernaturality and naturality alike – and loved women's flesh. Let all beauty be named and recognized as beauty.

A Lover would not deny the blackness of Jayne Mansfield – even tho he prefers his own madonna. To deny is to cancel a part of what love may be. I'm tired of voices of definition and denial.

The dark quality of Mansfield in each being should be cherished – even when there is only a trace – and she flows with it. Harlow and her quality are loved. We will carry Jean Harlow into Space, and Mansfield is still among us. For truth there must be liberty of all loves.

Man, free thinker, are you really solitary, reasoning
On earth where life shakes everything?
Your liberty is disposal of your forces

But the Universe is absent from your resolutions.

Respect an active spirit in the beast.
Each flower is a spirit-genius locked to Nature.
A love mystery lives in metal.
All is sensate! And everything is mighty on your being.

Beware in the blind wall a prying stare.
Matter is equipped with a voice!
– Don't make it serve a single impious use!

Often in a dark being lives a hidden god.
And like a newborn eye, covered by lids,
A pure spirit rises under the skin of stones.

– Gerard de Nerval

An eternal love-shot lies in all that's modern, and the hallu-cinations of pure beauty are as sizeless as a universe. Man and woman and child know their loves and hungers, and the irises and constellations are one thing. Cuba, and anger, and gold will not change or become less warm by lies.

Blackness, sexuality and freedom must not be denied in any shape – or they wither. Love and the Mysterious knock at the door! To deny any beauty is to deny a part of liberty – but everyone is free to do that. To deny any beauty is to deny a part of truth AND ALL DARK WHITE LOVELINESS!

SHAG

Tom Pickard

canny bord ower there
sharrap man yi think i nowt but tarts

divin na tho
wooden mind a bash arrit

hoo pet can a tek yi yem?
am a big streng lad
al luk after yi

a na ya not owld inuff ti suck a dummy

hoo lads tommys scored
whats ya name pet
howear gis a kiss
gis a bit feel pet
di yi fancy a meat injectin?
well jump on the end o this

suck me plums
gis a suck off

o yi commin fora walk wis?
will gan ower the quarry
a nas a shortcut

leave is alen

sharrap oral belt yi

grab a
gis a bit feel
pull a doon
lets have a bit tit
howear man am forst

am warnin yis al git the coppas

sharrap oral kick ya teeth in

pull a doon
rip a skort off
hurry up an stuff it tom
its me next

are man a cannit wait
stick it in the get
howld a doon
shi winnit keep still
well hit the twat
please keep still pet an a winnit be a minit
go on man go on

a-a-r-r-r thatsnice

howear well
its me next.

SOME WESTERN HAIKUS

Jack Kerouac

EXPLANATORY NOTE BY AUTHOR: The 'Haiku' was invented and developed over hundreds of years in Japan to be a complete poem in seventeen syllables and to pack in a whole vision of life in three short lines. A 'Western Haiku' need not concern itself with the seventeen syllables since Western languages cannot adapt themselves to the fluid syllabillic Japanese. I propose that the 'Western Haiku' simply say a lot in three short lines in any Western language.

Above all, a Haiku must be very simple and free of all poetic trickery and make a little picture and yet be as airy and graceful as a Vivaldi Pastorella. Here is a great Japanese Haiku that is simpler and prettier than any Haiku I could ever write in any language:-

> A day of quiet gladness, –
> Mount Fuji is veiled
> In misty rain.
> (Basho) (1644-1694)

Here is another:

Nesetsukeshi ko no
Sentaku ya natsu
No tsuki

She has put the child to sleep,
And now washes the clothes;
The summer moon.
(Issa) (1763-1827)

And another, by Buson (1715-1783):

The nightingale is singing,
Its small mouth
Open.

SOME WESTERN HAIKUS

Jack Kerouac

Arms folded
  to the moon,
Among the cows.

Birds singing
  in the dark
– Rainy dawn.

Elephants munching
  on grass – loving
Heads side by side.

Missing a kick
  at the icebox door
It closed anyway.

Perfect moonlit night
  marred
By family squabbles.

This July evening,
  a large frog
On my door sill.

Catfish fighting for his life,
  and winning,
Splashing us all.

Evening coming –
  the office girl
Unloosing her scarf.

The low yellow
  moon above the
Quiet lamplit house

Shall I say no?
  – fly rubbing
its back legs

Unencouraging sign
  –the fish store
Is closed.

Nodding against
  the wall, the flowers
Sneeze

Straining at the padlock,
  the garage doors
At noon

The taste
  of rain
–Why kneel?

The moon,
  the falling star
– Look elsewhere

The rain has filled
  the birdbath
Again, almost

And the quiet cat
  sitting by the post
Perceives the moon

Useless, useless,
  the heavy rain
Driving into the sea.

Juju beads on the
  Zen Manual:
My knees are cold.

Those birds sitting
  out there on the fence –
They're all going to die

The bottoms of my shoes
  are wet
from walking in the rain

In my medicine cabinet,
  the winter fly
has died of old age.

November – how nasal
  the drunken
Conductor's call

The moon had
  a cat's mustache
For a second

A big fat flake
  of snow
Falling all alone

The summer chair
  rocking by itself
In the blizzard

— from BOOK OF HAIKU

THE POEM

Semyon Kirsanov

A man.
  Inside,
he is weeping.
  A crumpled
envelope
  in his hand.

A hundred steps
  up, he moves
on the escalator.
  Up to the columns
and the bright hall
  – all kinds of men
are floating
  with lowered
heads
  up from the subway –

I see he is losing
  the ground
that was under
  his feet.
He is floating past
  marble wreaths
on the walls
  of this splendid
white vault . . .

  But he doesn't want
to see this
  marvelous hall

in motion.
   His eyes
– no one must notice! –
   are fighting
against the daggers
   of tears . . .
Should I
   go to him,
perhaps say –
   'Anything wrong?'

   No good.
No slow-moving talk
   is going to
help him.
   But perhaps –
poetry
   would?
A poem,
   rushing
hot to the rescue –
   to take away
grief,
   the burden
of worry,
   even the
greatest
   pain –

   to help him
get his foot back
   on the threshold
to make him
   rise
     back to life,

on the small stairs
   of its lines!

English Version by
Anselm Hollo

8.1.59

Pablo Picasso

On the new lush
grass at the
well-rim   a
careless young man
was sleeping all
most nude   wearing
skins of lamb or bear
next to the two or three
predetermined cardinal points
frog and partridge outside and in
side crumbs set to soak
next the oven
their muletas and silken
fabrics on top and
their table d'hôte dinners.
of metal and hard boiled
egg and faster and running
made hot coals and close
enuf to shoot a chicken and
a seam of split watermelon
hanging from every
crow.
nothing more
waiting for the tambourine and
the wing of a pine grove and

TOWERS OF THE ROSE DAWN

Philip Lamantia

Having lived
for a long time on each side of
the bridge within sight of three towers
it was only after the bridge fell
thunderously into the water
that a great wave rose

to carry me safely
before the four doors of the castle
and spill into my hands, a giant key
inscribed with the weir-image of the head & eyes
of a green and beautiful beast.

TROUT FISHING IN AMERICA

(A Novel)

Richard Brautigan

WORSEWICK

Worsewick Hot Springs was nothing fancy. Somebody put some boards across the creek. That was it.

The boards dammed up the creek enough to form a huge bathtub there, and the creek flowed over the top of the boards, invited like a postcard to the ocean a thousand miles away.

As I said Worsewick was nothing fancy, not like the places where the swells go. There were no buildings around. We saw an old shoe lying by the tub.

The hot springs came down off a hill and where they flowed there was a bright orange scum through the sage-brush. The hot springs flowed into the creek right there at the tub and that's where it was nice.

We parked our car on the dirt road and went down and took off our clothes, then we took off the baby's clothes and the deer-flies had at us until we got into the water, and then they stopped.

There was a green slime growing around the edges of the tub and there were dozens of dead fish floating in our bath. Their bodies had been turned white by death, like frost on iron doors. Their eyes were large and stiff.

The fish had made the mistake of going down the creek too far and ending up in hot water, singing, 'When you lose your money, learn to lose.'

We played and relaxed in the water. The green slime and the dead fish played and relaxed with us and flowed out over us and entwined themselves about us.

Splashing around in that hot water with my woman, I began to get ideas, as they say. After a while I placed my body in such a position in the water that the baby could not see my hard-on.

I did this by going deeper and deeper in the water, like a dinosaur, and letting the green slime and dead fish cover me over.

My woman took the baby out of the water and gave her a bottle and put her back in the car. The baby was tired. It was *really* time for her to take a nap.

My woman took a blanket out of the car and covered up the windows that faced the hot springs. She put the blanket on top of the car and then lay rocks on the blanket to hold it in place. I remember her standing there by the car.

Then she came back to the water, and the deerflies were at her, and then it was my turn. After a while she said, 'I don't have my diaphragm with me and besides it wouldn't work in the water, anyway. I think it's a good idea if you don't come inside me. What do you think?'

I thought this over and said all right. I didn't want any more kids for a long time. The green slime and dead fish were all about our bodies.

I remember a dead fish floated under her neck. I waited for it to come up on the other side, and it came up on the other side.

Worsewick was nothing fancy.

Then I came, and just cleared her in a split second like an airplane in the movies, pulling out of a nosedive and sailing over the roof of a school.

My sperm came out into the water, unaccustomed to the light, and instantly it became a misty, stringy kind of thing and swirled out like a falling star, and I saw a dead fish come forward and float into my sperm, bending it in the middle. His eyes were stiff like iron.

THE SALT CREEK COYOTES

High and lonesome and steady, it's the smell of sheep down in the valley that has done it to them. Here all afternoon in the

129

rain I've been listening to the sound of the coyotes up on Salt Creek.

The smell of the sheep grazing in the valley has done it to them. Their voices water and come down the canyon, past the summer homes. Their voices are a creek, running down the mountain, over the bones of sheep, living and dead.

O, THERE ARE COYOTES UP ON SALT CREEK so the sign on the trial says, and it also says, WATCH OUT FOR CYANIDE CAPSULES PUT ALONG THE CREEK TO KILL COYOTES. DON'T PICK THEM UP AND EAT THEM. NOT UNLESS YOU'RE A COYOTE. THEY'LL KILL YOU. LEAVE THEM ALONE.

Then the sign says this all over again in Spanish.

!AH! HAY COYOTES EN SALT CREEK, TAMBIEN. CUIDADO CON LAS CAPSULAS DE CIANUDO: MATAN. NO LAS COMA, A MENOS QUE SEA VD. UN COYOTE. MATAN. NO LAS TOQUE.

It does not say it in Russian.

I asked an old guy in a bar about those cyanide capsules up on Salt Creek and he told me that they were a kind of pistol. They put a pleasing coyote scent on the trigger (probably the smell of a coyote snatch) and then a coyote comes along and gives it a good sniff, a fast feel and BLAM! That's all, brother.

I went fishing up on Salt Creek and caught a nice little Dolly Varden trout, spotted and slender as a snake you'd expect to find in a jewelry store, but after a while I could think only of the gas chamber at San Quentin.

O Caryl Chessman and Alexander Robillard Vistas! as if they were names for tracts of three-bedroom houses with wall-to-wall carpets and plumbing that defies the imagination.

Then it came to me up there on Salt Creek, capital punishment being what it is, an act of state business with no song down the railroad track after the train has gone and no vibration on the rails, that they should take the head of a coyote killed by one of those God-damn cyanide things up on Salt Creek and hollow it out and dry it in the sun and then make it into a crown with the teeth running in a circle around the top of it and a nice green light coming off the teeth.

Then the witnesses and newspapermen and gas chamber flunkies would have to watch a king wearing a coyote crown die there in front of them, the gas rising in the chamber like a rain mist drifting down the mountain from Salt Creek. It has been raining here now for two days, and through the trees, the heart stops beating.

A HALF SUNDAY HOMAGE TO A WHOLE LEONARDO DA VINCI

On this funky winter day in rainy San Francisco I've had a vision of Leonardo da Vinci. My woman's out slaving away, no day off, working on Sunday. She left here at eight o'clock this morning for Powell and California. I've been sitting here ever since like a toad on a log dreaming about Leonardo da Vinci.

I dreamt he was on the South Bend Tackle Company payroll, but of course, he was wearing different clothes and speaking with a different accent and possessor of a different childhood, perhaps an American childhood spent in a town like Lordsburg, New Mexico, or Winchester, Virginia.

I saw him inventing a new spinning lure for trout fishing in America. I saw him first of all working with his imagination, then with metal and color and hooks, trying a little of this and a little of that, and then adding motion and then taking it away and then coming back again with a different motion, and in the end the lure was invented.

He called his bosses in. They looked at the lure and all fainted. Alone, standing over their bodies, he held the lure in his hand and gave it a name. He called it *The Last Supper*. Then he went about waking up his bosses.

In a matter of months that trout fishing lure was the sensation of the Twentieth Century, far outstripping such shallow accomplishments as Hiroshima or Mahatma Gandi. Millions of *Last Suppers* were sold in America. The Vatican ordered ten thousand and they didn't even have any trout there.

Testimonials poured in. Thirty-four ex-presidents of the United States all said, 'I caught my limit on *The Last Supper*'.

131

Lawrence Ferlinghetti

Heaven

        was only half as far that night

at the poetry recital

        listening to the burnt phrases

when I heard the poet have

        a rhyming erection

then took away with a

        lost look

'Every animal' he said at last

    'After intercourse is sad'

        But the back-row lovers
        looked oblivious

           and glad

GREENWICH VILLAGE
SUICIDE

Gregory Corso

Arms outstretched
Hands flat against the windowsides
She looks down
Thinks of Bartok, Van Gogh
And New Yorker cartoons
She falls

They take her away with a Daily News on her face
And a storekeeper throws hot water on the sidewalk

BABI YAR

Yevgeny Yevtushenko

Babi Yar
has no mausoleum.
Catacomb
is this ravine.
I stand here, afraid
surrounded by death.
I stand here, old
as a Jew,
as the Jew
crucified!
see my hands,
crucified! Dreyfus
howled at
spewed upon
by a mob
of judges,
imprisoned, walled in
insulted, beaten.
   Women
   in sweet frilly dresses
   poking their parasols
   in my face.
   Shrieking
   with hate.
I stand here
I am the kid
in Byolostok

watching the puddle
of the blood on the floor
the tough guys have spilled,
their vodka
cursing us
in their veins
making them deaf
to everything but
that roar:
   BEAT THE KIKES!
   KEEP RUSSIA CLEAN!
   They take
   the boot
   to my mother.
O you Russians
you never held
with such things as frontiers
and creeds
to divide one man
from another.
But those among you
who soiled their hands crimson
have often shouted
your name –
the Russian people: yes
'The Russian People's League'
– a bunch
of haters!
I stand here
I am Ann Frank
a green twig
of a girl, as easy
to tear
off the flowering branch,
of love, of her love
that was natural
and a fullness.
I stand here
   I look at you
   at myself
   it is hard to see

anything, other
trees, no trees, no
leaves, no sky
– but this rushing
sound in our ears –
– the boots –
already?
No, it is April
Coming to find us out,
mouth against mouth
in a small dark room . . .
– but who
is that –
rapping against
the door –
No, it is the river.
Breaking
to flow
with Spring. . . .
It is very quiet now
as I stand here.
Inside me
someone
is howling,
silently,
over the whispering grass
under the tall trees.
The trees
are judges
in black.
I take off my cap
to see
my hair turning gray,
and the howl
inside me
pushes out
through my pores! for
the millions,
who lie here,
faceless.
I stand here

I lie here
an old man
snuffed out
by the machine-gun's
deadly spout
a young man
who had
a wife
a young wife
who had a
son
snuffed out
by the spurting lead
They have entered
my skin, these people
my veins
and my bones,
they have made my body their catacomb.
They were Jews.
And this place cannot hear
The International's
fierce booming voice
until the last hater
of these people
lies covered
with earth,
this place
will be deaf
to that song.
I stand here
I was not born
a Jew
but those
who hated
and hate
the blood
that was shed here
– they hate
me, as I
have hated them
all my life,

and that
is what makes me
a Russian.

–1961

*English Version by
Anselm Hollo*

A SUPERMARKET IN CALIFORNIA

Allen Ginsberg

What thoughts I have of you tonight, Walt Whitman, for I walked down the sidestreets under the trees with a headache self-conscious looking at the full moon.

In my hungry fatigue, and shopping for images, I went into the neon fruit supermarket, dreaming of your enumerations!

What peaches and what penumbras! Whole families shopping at night! Aisles full of husbands! Wives in the avocados, babies in the tomatoes! – and you, Garcia Lorca, what were you doing down by the watermelons?

I saw you, Walt Whitman, childless, lonely old grubber, poking among the meats in the refrigerator and eyeing the grocery boys.

I heard you asking questions of each: Who killed the pork chops? What price bananas? Are you my Angel?

I wandered in and out of the brilliant stacks of cans following you, and followed in my imagination by the store detective.

We strode down the open corridors together in our solitary fancy tasting artichokes, possessing every frozen delicacy, and never passing the cashier.

Where are we going, Walt Whitman? The doors close in an hour. Which way does your beard point tonight?

(I touch your book and dream of our odyssey in the supermarket and feel absurd.)

Will we walk all night through solitary streets? The trees add shade to shade, lights out in the houses, we'll both be lonely.

Will we stroll dreaming of the lost America of love past blue automobiles in driveways, home to our silent cottage?

Ah, dear father, graybeard, lonely old courage-teacher, what America did you have when Charon quit poling his ferry and you got out on a smoking bank and stood watching the boat disappear on the black waters of Lethe?

Berkeley 1955

140

THEOLOGY

Michael Horowitz

God's in His Heaven
　　Creating Earth –
When He gets down here
　　He's going to raise Hell